Anything But Easy

A Memoir of a Special-Needs Adoption from China

Marie Spiess

ISBN: 1452843988
ISBN-13: 9781452843988
Library of Congress Control Number: 2010906332

To my husband, Kyle, because without your

love and support none of this would

have been possible.

And to all

orphaned children

waiting for their forever families.

Contents

Introduction

I was already a mom to two healthy boys. Life was good—I should have been perfectly happy. For months I tried to ignore the burning desire for a third child that sat in the pit of my stomach. I pushed away the thoughts about adoption that seemed to keep popping up in the back of my brain. Finally, after about a year, I couldn't deny myself any longer. In the spring of 2006, my husband and I embarked on the ultimate journey of adoption.

We started out in the China nonspecial-needs program, but as the wait time continued to lengthen, we explored special-needs adoption. Before that, I had never considered special needs—the words had a negative connotation for me. In my mind, these were children with major medical and emotional issues who would never lead a normal life. They would require twenty-four-hour care; I didn't have it in me. As it turns out, I was completely wrong. The more we investigated, the more we realized that many of the special-needs children from overseas had very correctable problems; with that realization, my preconceptions disappeared. Within months we shifted gears and went full speed ahead into the world of special-needs adoption, and we have never looked back. As with many things in life, our adoption journey took several unexpected twists and turns. Overall, it went well, but attachment and bonding proved to be more difficult than we'd hoped. Dealing with a toddler who had lived only in an orphanage took an emotional toll. It took perseverance, determination, a lot of love, and a few tears along the way, but the prize at the finish line was a happy family.

I feel that every child deserves to live with a family, to love, and be loved. Adoption, whether domestic or international, is a wonderful thing. There are speed bumps along the way, and I have shared these private details to help prepare those families that are considering adoption. Be warned; once you are touched by adoption, and see what changes occur when a child is loved, you won't want to stop there. In the future you may find yourself becoming an adoption advocate. We have found that adoption was one of the most challenging and rewarding ventures we will ever encounter.

I hope that you will enjoy reading about our journey.

Marie Spiess

CHAPTER 1

The Decision

It was a typical Friday morning at our house. I was getting ready for work, and as I was drying my hair, a sharp abdominal pain hit me. It didn't last long but was enough to get my attention and make me sit down.

I was pregnant with our second child, and my due date was in three days. As I sat there on the side of the bathtub, I had to wonder, *Was that a contraction?* I finished getting myself and our two-year-old son, Mason, ready to go. I dropped him off at the sitter's house and had no further pains.

I was almost at work when the pain returned. This time it was stronger and lasted longer. I gripped the steering wheel tight with both hands until the pain subsided. Now I was getting excited. *Was this baby coming today?* I made it to work with no further contractions, and I excitedly told my coworkers that this could be the day.

I work as a physician assistant (PA) for a surgical practice, and that day I was seeing patients in the office. The location was very convenient as our office is directly connected to the hospital where I was to deliver my baby. I began seeing patients, and the pains started coming more frequently but the timing was erratic. I remember pacing in my office between patients, still not believing this was "it" because my first child had to be induced and still took nearly a day to show his beautiful face. By 10:30 A.M., it was getting difficult to see patients. I was finding it very challenging to concentrate on what the patient was saying as I was having contractions.

I finally called my husband, Kyle, at work and told him he should leave work and head to my office. The contractions were coming every two to ten minutes but still very irregular. I called my obstetrician's office, and they said to go home and relax since the contractions were not regular. We lived about thirty minutes from the hospital and knowing my own body pretty well, I decided to stay right at work. However, Kyle worked forty-five minutes away. By the time he arrived, I was in such pain I couldn't even walk. He couldn't believe I waited so long to call him, but up until that point I still wasn't sure it was the real thing.

Kyle put me in a wheelchair and to the hospital we went. Things were happening so fast we didn't even take the time to call our parents. With every contraction, I became more excited, as we were about to meet our second child. By the time we arrived at the labor and delivery unit, I was very uncomfortable. I already knew many of the OB nurses as I've worked at this hospital for several years. Seeing me so uncomfortable, they got me right into a delivery room, and when they checked my cervix, I was already dilated to seven centimeters! Things moved quickly after that. I was starting to push before I was even formally checked in to the hospital.

Fortunately, my doctor was able to arrive in time for the delivery. The baby's heartbeat was being monitored, and as I was pushing, the heart rate started to slow; it was imperative to deliver him as soon as possible. Even through the pain, I knew this was a dangerous situation and fear swept over me. Without much hesitation, the doctor utilized a vacuum-assisted delivery to facilitate a speedy birth. Moments later our son was born at 2:00 P.M. on July 23, 2004. He was a healthy baby boy, and we named him Max.

The delivery happened so quickly, Kyle and I were in shock. We looked at each other in disbelief, and we couldn't help but to smile and laugh. I felt great. My husband and I sat there in bed with our newest addition to the family. We were giddy with excitement, still in disbelief that it happened so fast. Max seemed so content. Kyle took some pictures and called our parents.

Shortly after that moment, I remember sitting in bed feeling powerless. All of a sudden it was like someone flipped a switch, and I started feeling lightheaded and weak. I told Kyle I wasn't feeling well. I think he thought the events of the day were catching up with me and that I was probably just tired. The nurse said it was time to get up and try to urinate; then they would take me to a new private room across the hall from the delivery room that I was in. The nurse and Kyle helped me out of bed, and I felt very weak, but I made it to the bathroom, which was only a few steps away. I sat on the toilet, and I was so faint it was difficult to talk. The nurse was cooing over Max, and she commented on how much I was urinating. I muttered, "I'm not peeing." I remember the alarmed look on her face as she came over to me. Her eyes widened—I was hemorrhaging. She quickly tried to get me up off the toilet to the wheelchair. She and Kyle pulled me up, and that's all I remember. Everything went black.

I regained consciousness as they were wheeling me into my new room. Fortunately, with the use of medications, the bleeding stopped but not before I lost a significant amount of blood. Based on the results of my lab work, I lost about half my blood volume. For the next week, I was too lightheaded and weak to walk for more than a few feet at a time. I even had to sit down to take a shower, and when I was done, I was exhausted.

Kyle was very busy that first week after we came home from the hospital. I tried to help with the kids, but let's face it, I wasn't much help at all. He did a great job of taking care of all of us. After a few more weeks, I was starting to feel back to my old self again. Max was doing great, and Mason seemed to enjoy his new role as a big brother. We were a happy family of four. We always said that we only wanted two kids, so here we were—our pseudo perfect family.

As Max began to outgrow some of his baby items, the reality that there wouldn't be any more babies to wear these clothes and play with the toys hit me. He wasn't even a year old, and I started to feel the desire for a third child. *It would be nice to have a girl*, I thought. I mentioned the idea to Kyle. His original reaction was a deer in the headlights look. Then he responded with, "I thought you said you only wanted two kids." Apparently he forgot about a woman's prerogative to change her mind. We had a few very brief discussions on the matter, but Kyle held firm. "Why would I want to chance losing you and having to raise three kids by myself?" Even though my postpartum bleeding was a relatively minor issue on most counts, it was enough of a reality check that things do sometimes go wrong. I understood his reasoning and realized that getting pregnant may have proved difficult anyway.

I had no troubles conceiving Mason, but we tried for over a year to conceive Max. I had one miscarriage at eight weeks, which was very discouraging after trying for so many months. I was fortunate to get pregnant with Max with the use of a medication called Clomid. I guess it was a combination of Kyle's fears and my questionable fertility that made me start to think about adoption. I honestly don't know where I got the idea. I didn't know anyone who'd adopted, and in our small, rural Michigan town, it was something definitely outside of the norm. Maybe it was one of those Dave Thomas Foundation TV specials promoting foster adoption or a documentary about orphaned children in other countries that planted the seed. Those shows always left me teary. I powered up the computer, went online, and started researching adoption.

The more I read, the more intrigued I became. Adopting made complete sense to me. We were blessed with two biological children; why not adopt a child already here in this world who needed a family? I was sure that I wanted to adopt, so one day I said to Kyle, "What do you think about us adopting?" I got that same deer in the headlights look. This time followed by silence. Then, "Where did you get that idea?" He didn't say yes or no, or for that matter much of anything. As he puts it now, adoption wasn't anything he'd ever thought about or considered before.

We did a bit more research about adopting, but Max was only twelve-months-old, so we didn't feel rushed to do anything at that time. However, once Max turned two, adopting a third child was something I couldn't stop thinking about. I read everything I could get my hands on that had anything to do with adoption. At first, the

fees associated with adoption seemed unobt
with a little more investigating, we learr
United States government provides a signifi
tax credit, as well as a much smaller one from the state ᴏ
Michigan. Larger corporations often provide adoption assistance funding, and sure enough, my husband's company
provided that benefit to its workers. When we took those
credits and assistance into consideration, the fees no longer
seemed so overwhelming.

We researched the adoption agencies in our area,
and discussed what type of adoption we wanted to pursue. There are many options regarding adopting a child,
including the decision to adopt domestically (children
from your home country) or internationally. If you choose
domestic, will it be through foster care or privately ar-
ranged? Will you choose an open or closed adoption? If
international, which country? With either domestic or international, would you want to adopt an infant or older
child? Would you consider only one who is healthy or are
you open to one who has special needs? The decisions can
be overwhelming. For Kyle and me this decision was one
of the easiest.

Financing Your Adoption

A recent poll taken by *Adoptive Families* magazine found that the average cost of adoption is $25,000. At first glance, that figure may seem overwhelming. Here are some resources and tips:

- Federal Adoption Tax Credit: Although the amount changes yearly, the maximum adoption tax credit for the year 2010 is $13,170 for qualified adoption expenses, including travel. Most states also offer a much smaller tax credit as well. Check with your accountant for the latest adoption tax credits or go to www.irs.gov for more information.

- Savings and Loans: Many families have utilized home equity loans as they generally have a lower interest rate than a personal loan.

- Fund-raising: Fund-raising throughout your community or church may also help defray the costs. People are usually happy to help for such a wonderful cause.

- Employer Subsidy: Some employers offer adoption assistance as a part of the benefits package. Call your human resources department and ask if your company provides adoption assistance.

For suggestions on how to approach your employer about adoption benefits, check out the following Web sites.

www.davethomasfoundation.org

www.adoptivefamilies.com

When we decided on an agency, we were required to attend informational meetings, and it was at one of those meetings that I heard the statistic that for every baby born in the United States that will be adopted, there are thirty perspective couples. Nearly all of these couples were dealing with infertility. Kyle and I were blessed to already have two healthy biological children, so this clearly was not the path for us as there were too many other couples that needed these children much more than us. We knew we wanted a little girl to complete our family, and that's why adopting from China was the perfect answer for our family.

In 1979 the Chinese officials enacted the one-child law in an attempt to control the population growth in China. This law is the very reason so many girls were available for adoption. In traditional Chinese culture, it is desirable to have a son. The thinking behind this is a son will eventually take care of his parents when they become elderly. When daughters marry, they help their husbands care for his parents. Thus, if a couple's firstborn is a girl, she may possibly be abandoned in hopes that the next pregnancy would produce a son. If a family was found to have more than one child, they could be heavily fined—up to six times their annual income. The one-child law has recently been relaxed, but there are many people who live in poverty, and feeding and caring for another child is just not an option, especially if the child was born with a medical problem. It is illegal to abandon children in China, so it is very rare that the child would be left with a note or even a birth date. It's hard for me to understand how difficult it must be for these mothers to abandon their babies, but I do believe they hope for a better life for these children and often place them in very public locations, so that they will be quickly found and cared for. Because of the above, nearly all the children available for nonspecial needs adoption were girls, and they were usually twelve- to eighteen-months-old at the time of adoption. We wanted to adopt a child as young as possible to preserve our children's birth order. So given the above factors, adopting from China was the perfect fit for us.

Picking an Adoption Agency

The best way to find an adoption agency in your area is to go online and search for *licensed international adoption agencies* within your state. From there, you can research which agencies deal with adoptions from China. Most agencies offer a free initial consultation or informational meeting; utilize these to decide which agency will be best for you. Once you pick an agency, they will become your mentor as they assist you through each step of the adoption process. Many agencies are a "one-stop shop," offering home-study evaluations, dossier preparation, travel arrangements, post-placement reports, etc. Hiring a lawyer for a China adoption is not usually necessary.

CHAPTER 2

The Paperwork Chase

It was May 2006, when we made the ultimate decision that, yes, we wanted to adopt a little girl from China. Max was nearly two-years-old. We waited to tell everyone our decision to adopt until we were 100 percent sure. This was a very private and personal decision that was ours. I'm glad we stuck with that decision because not everyone was as excited for us as we'd hoped. It's not that anyone thought it was a bad thing, but this was different, unchartered territory. One family member flat out said, "Why would you want to do that? You've got two healthy kids already. Isn't that enough for you?" That comment was hurtful at first, but I realized it was just out of concern for Kyle and me. The great majority of family and friends embraced the idea of our adoption with open arms. My husband is one of four boys, and at that time, there were five grandchildren in the family—all boys. The thought of having a girl in the family was very exciting for Kyle's side of the family.

We were required to attend several informational meetings and do "homework" on adoption. Most of the readings and workbooks were related to attachment and bonding with your child. While we were working on our "homework," we were busy preparing our dossier to send to China. A dossier is a set of all the documents required by the U.S. and Chinese governments to complete an international adoption. China Center of Adoption Affairs (CCAA) requires *several* documents from prospective adoptive families. We had to write an adoption petition and provide letters from employers with our wages, letters from local police stating we were law-abiding citizens, official copies of our birth and marriage certificates, medical exams, a financial statement, and letters of personal reference. Keep in mind, each one of these documents had to be perfectly signed and notarized. In addition to all of those documents, we had to file for official paperwork through the United States government, which required us to be fingerprinted. With any adoption, a home study is also required. In a home study, a social worker from the adoption agency comes into the home and interviews the entire family. The intent of this study is to make sure we are able to provide a safe home for a child. I've heard many families become very stressed out about the home study, but with two little boys and one large golden retriever, our house was already childproof. In addition to the large stack of notarized documents mentioned above, there was another whole list of documents and photos that also were included. Once the entire dossier was complete, our caseworker reviewed it; it was then translated and sent to China (finally) in October 2006. What a sense of relief when the dossier was sent! Now the waiting began.

We had signed up for the nonspecial-needs program. At that time, the wait until referral of a child was approximately twelve months, and then we would travel six to eight weeks after the referral arrived. Just a year earlier the wait time until referral was just over six months, so twelve months seemed like a long time, but we had two busy children at home to keep us occupied.

Unfortunately, the wait time went from bad to worse and was steadily increasing in length. If the current pace continued, it would be at least another two years before we would travel to China. (As I write this book the wait time is closer to four to five years.) We had wanted our children to be somewhat close in age, but at this rate, our second child would already be in school when we adopted our one-year-old. Families around the world waiting for a referral became disappointed.

We were approximately six months into the wait when someone asked us if we'd given any thought to the special-needs program. My initial reaction was that it wasn't for us. Somewhere in my mind, I had thought all the children in the special needs program had major medical problems. As a mom of soon-to-be three children and working full time, I didn't feel I had the time to devote to a child with intensive special needs and care.

Eligibility Requirements to Adopt from China

On May 1, 2007, China Center of Adoption Affairs (CCAA) enforced new eligibility regulations for prospective adoptive parents. The list is fairly extensive and an abbreviated list is included below:

- The prospective couple (man and woman) must be in a stable marriage of at least two years. If either person has had a previous marriage (not more than two), they must be married for five years.

- Both husband and wife must be between the ages of 30 and 50. For a special-needs child, they may be between the ages of 30 and 55.

- Both must be in excellent physical and mental health. The following conditions would make the couple ineligible:

  - AIDS, mental disability, blindness even in one eye, hearing loss (those adopting a special-needs child with the same condition are exempt), dysfunction of the arms or legs, severe facial deformity, serious diseases that require long-term treatment such as cancer, lupus, epilepsy, chronic kidney disease, etc. Also included is a major organ transplant less than ten years ago, schizophrenia, medication for mental disorders, including depression and anxiety if stopped less than two years ago, and last but not least, each parent must have a body mass index (BMI) less than 40.

- Both husband and wife must have a clean criminal history. This includes any incidents of violence, or drug or alcohol abuse.

- Both should have an education at or above the level of high school senior.

- Husband or wife should have a stable occupation. The family annual income should be $10,000 for each family member, and the family net assets should be $80,000 or greater.

- The number of children in the family under the age of 18 years should be less than five, and the youngest should have reached the age of one. Adoption of a special-needs child is exempt from this regulation.

We then learned that nearly 70 percent of children in China that are available for adoption have some type of special need. Many of these special needs children have minor correctable problems. For example, if a baby had an umbilical hernia, he would be considered a special-needs child. Now we were intrigued. I could deal with minor to moderate medical issues—after all, I was a PA.

Special-needs adoptions happen much faster as you are matched with a specific child, but the children were often older, which wasn't a major issue for us as long as she was younger than Max. Preserving the birth order was something we wanted, but it was also a policy of our adoption agency. We learned that our agency received a new list of special-needs children every five to six months.

The list would include a photo of each child with his or her birth date, and a very brief description of the child's medical problem. The medical problems could range from something as minor as a large birthmark to missing limbs, heart disease, hepatitis, etc.

Our caseworker signed us up to be in the group to view the special-needs referrals. Now we were excited all over again at the thought of potentially matching with our daughter in the next month or so! Our caseworker informed us that the list would be e-mailed to all of the waiting families in the special-needs group. We then would have a few days to contact the caseworkers if we were interested in any of the children. After the deadline passed, the caseworkers would sit down and review the inquiries for each child. The family who had waited the longest would get more detailed information on the child and then take approximately two days to make a decision if they wanted to adopt that child. If they chose not to adopt that child, the information would then be passed down to the next waiting family. Needless to say, I checked my e-mail several times every day.

CHAPTER 3

It's Really Happening: Receiving a Referral

It was April 2007 when our agency received the next group of special-needs referrals. There was no warning. One day I opened my e-mail, and there it was, staring me right in the face. It was a group of thirteen children, both boys and girls. They varied greatly in age and medical problems. For each child, there was a small photo, under which, was the child's birth date, province where he or she was located, and a very brief three to four word description of the special need/medical condition. There were three little girls on that list that were younger than Max. They all had very different medical issues.

I printed the e-mail and that night Kyle and I lay in bed carefully studying the tiny pictures wondering, *Could we be looking at our daughter?* The next day, we informed our caseworker that we would like more information on all three of the girls. We were e-mailed files on all three girls with more medical information, but it was still limited at best. We had two days to make a final request for a child on the list.

As we studied each file closely, Kyle proclaimed, "This is the one—she's got the same birthday as my dad." She did indeed. It was our sign. Many families that have adopted feel that they were destined for their specific child. Her Chinese name was Zhuge Juanzi. The agency assigned temporary names to each child; I believe this is to avoid confusion with pronunciations of the Chinese names. This little girl's agency name was Mya. She was born with a cleft lip and palate, and only the lip had been repaired. She was twenty-two-months-old—only eleven months younger than Max. So much for our concerns about our children's ages being too far apart! She was one of the few that had a smile in her photo.

The next two days we tried to learn as much as possible about cleft lip and palate. By now, Kyle and I were starting to grow attached to the idea that this could be our daughter. Since we didn't originally start the adoption process with the intention of adopting a special-needs child, this had to be a mutual decision. Life is never predictable. Anytime a woman gets pregnant, she and her partner think they are going to have a healthy baby, but the reality is it doesn't always work that way. We could adopt a "healthy" child to later find out she has a medical condition. This child had a cleft lip and palate, which are correctable problems. Would it take several surgeries and intensive speech therapy? Sure, but these were very obtainable things.

After mulling over 100 scenarios in my mind, I was sure I wanted to proceed with our request for Mya. I didn't push Kyle at all as parenting three young children requires teamwork. In order for us to be the best team possible, we both needed to be comfortable with our decision. She was all I could think about day and night. I knew in my heart that this was meant to be, but was scared to grow too attached to the idea. The night before the deadline, we lay in bed once again looking at the thirteen innocent faces on my sheet of paper. Our eyes kept landing on Mya and her diagnosis of cleft lip and palate. Kyle said, "We can deal with that, so let's do it." I excitedly turned to him and asked him, "Are you sure?" about a hundred times. Each time his response was, "Yes."

Figure 1: Kaia's referral photograph.

I don't think I slept at all that night because I was so excited. I had only positive thoughts as I imagined how our family would change, the joy she would bring our family, and how she would blossom into a beautiful, successful woman. With great excitement, the first thing the next morning I contacted our agency and informed them, "We want Mya!"

Our caseworker informed me that the procedure would be as follows: The agency would have a meeting to review all requests for each child. The family that had been waiting the longest would get the referral. That family would then have one week to make a final decision after reviewing the complete file. If that family chose not to adopt, then she would be offered to the next family. I was told that a decision would be made in the next few days.

I was skeptical. I knew that there were many families that had been waiting much longer than us. We tried not to get excited, knowing full well that we'd be crushed if she were matched to another family. The next day at work, I held my breath every time the phone rang, hoping it was the adoption agency. The first day passed with no phone call. The second day went with no phone call. By the third morning Kyle and I had figured it probably wasn't going to work out the way we had hoped. I probably would have called our caseworker that morning, but as fate would have it, we were busy preparing to leave for a trip to Florida. I was scheduled to attend a medical conference in Tampa, Florida, just a short drive from where Kyle's brother and his wife lived. We were able to turn my week-long conference into a much-needed family vacation.

It was mid-afternoon on a Friday, and we were in line to board the plane to Florida when I heard my cell phone ring. It was a message from one of my coworkers telling me that our adoption agency had called looking for me. The caseworker told my office that she would send me an e-mail if I couldn't reach her before 5:00 P.M. So here we were, about to board our plane that wouldn't touch down in Florida until after 5:00 P.M. on Friday. My heart raced with excitement. *Could this be the phone call we've been waiting for, or the phone call to tell us Mya was offered to another family?*

I dialed our caseworker's number as fast as I could. Her secretary answered and put me on hold as our caseworker was speaking to another family. I waited and I waited for what seemed like an eternity. My heart was pounding, and my mind was racing. Her secretary kept asking if I wanted to keep holding. I tried to get information from the secretary but to no avail. I sat on hold until the flight attendant announced all cell phones were to be turned off. Crushed, there we were, on a flight to Florida with the future of our adoption hanging on the wings. I was somewhat of a basket case during the whole flight wondering what if? Fortunately, we had two small children with us that we desperately tried to keep occupied and quiet, so that helped to keep my mind off the e-mail waiting to be read as soon as I could get my hands on a computer.

The flight went well, but by the time we landed, our boys were getting hungry and restless. To make matters worse, the car rental agency had all of our paperwork messed up, so it was well after 5:00 P.M. before we were enroute to my brother-in-law's house. When we arrived, we exchanged hugs and then quickly asked, "Where's your computer?" As they looked a little confused, we quickly filled them in about the news awaiting us. The computer was in the kitchen. I logged on and sure enough, there was a message from our caseworker. Kyle stood next to me as we opened and read the message together. The message read:

Hi Marie,

I am excited to let you know that if you and your husband are interested in Mya, we can put her on hold for you. I left you a message at your work number but was not sure if you would be able to call me back before 5:00 p.m. You can give me a call on Monday to let me know what you are thinking.

We will be in touch.

Our prayers had been answered! We hugged as tears of joy ran down our faces. First thing Monday morning, we contacted our agency with our answer—"Yes, we of course want to proceed with adopting Mya." We were officially matched with our soon-to-be daughter! There was yet more paperwork to process related to a special-needs adoption, as well as work on our letter of intent that would be sent to China. We were able to complete most of it from Florida that first week, but we were told the wait would be yet another seven to nine months. While in Florida, we called our parents to share the good news and we sent out a mass e-mail to our closest friends and family. With the help of Kyle's brother, we set up an online journal that we later used to keep everyone informed about the developments during the adoption process.

Online Adoption Journals

Friends and family members are interested in your adoption. Keeping them informed can be an overwhelming task. There are several Web sites that offer prospective adoptive families a place to keep an online journal. The journal is password protected, so only those people whom you invite can see your journal. Once you register and set up your online journal, you can make entries as frequently as you wish, and one of the nice features is your readers can comment and share their thoughts with you, too. Below are some Web sites that offer this service, but also check with your adoption agency as they may provide this service.

www.blogger.com

www.my-diary.org

www.typepad.com

www.wordpress.com

www.youbelong.net

CHAPTER 4

The Waiting Game

Over the next several weeks, I started to research and read as much information as I could get my hands on. I tried to learn as much as possible about cleft lip and palate, but the medical information we had on Mya was minimal at best. Some of the medical reports were conflicting; one report read that both the cleft lip and palate had been repaired. We requested more information, but we were told the likelihood of receiving any more information was low. Then one day, through the power of the Internet, I found a Yahoo group for adoptive families that had adopted from Ningxia, the province where our daughter lived.

This group proved to be a great find. I learned more about Mya's province and orphanage through it than any other source. Our agency had not had any families travel to this orphanage before, so we felt like we were in unchartered territories. She was located in Yinchuan city, Ningxia province of China. It was a very small province in northern China along the Yellow River. We were informed that this was an autonomous region with a large number of minorities living there, many of which are Muslim. I will never know for sure if what we were told was accurate, but we were informed the orphanage housed approximately 200 children and most of them had special needs. The minority populations did not have to follow the one-child law, but the area was largely agricultural and families could not afford to care for children with medical problems. That was the major reason most of these children were abandoned. From native Chinese I learned that these children with medical problems were considered bad luck. The idea that these innocent children could be considered bad luck and undesirable was heartbreaking for me to hear. The Yahoo group consisted of only fifty-five people— small by comparison to other Yahoo orphanage groups in China. There were families from around the world that had adopted from Yinchuan, and I was pleased and relieved that these families had very positive things to say about the caretakers at the orphanage. That group was a wealth of information, and I will always be grateful to them.

Virtual Support Groups at YahooGroups

Other families who are going through the adoption process and/or have already adopted can be a great source of information. YahooGroups are online groups that have a common interest, and there are many related to adoption.

To find potential groups go to groups.yahoo.com, and in the search box enter terms such as *China adoption*, *China special-needs adoption*, or more specifically, the name of the orphanage where your child is living.

On May 21, just one day after my birthday, I received a wonderful surprise in my e-mail. It was a message from our agency with an updated photo of our little girl. She looked so much older than the referral photos, and she looked much healthier, too, as her cheeks looked fuller. Apparently, the agency had requested updated photos of the children as some of the children looked a little on the thin side in the original referral photos. This new photo brought a whole new sense of excitement and a realization that she wasn't a baby; she was already a toddler. We studied the photo intensely and sent it to everyone we knew. I was curious how she was doing developmentally, but it was impossible to tell if she were standing or sitting in the photograph.

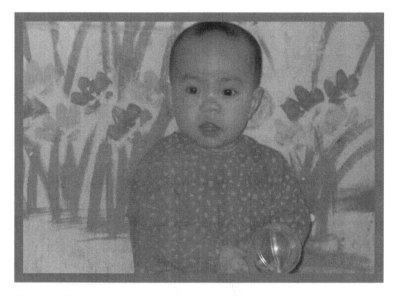

Figure 2: Updated photograph of our daughter.

It was now June, and we still hadn't decided on a name for our daughter. This wasn't uncommon for us as after Max was born, it took us until right before discharge from the hospital until we were sure about his name. Kyle had a favorite name for a girl, as did I, but unfortunately we didn't approve of each other's first choice. We went on a camping trip that weekend and gave ourselves the deadline to pick a name by the end of the weekend. We individually went through a book of baby names and wrote down a list of suitable names. Sitting around the campfire at night, we looked at each other's lists and vetoed the ones we didn't like. By the end of the weekend, we had it narrowed down and we agreed that Kaia (pronounced Ki-ya) Juanzi Spiess would be her name. Juanzi (which sounds like Jenza) was her given Chinese name, and thus we chose to keep that as a part of her legal name.

Kaia's second birthday was on June 20, and she would definitely still be in China for her birthday. We wanted to do something special for her, but we were still waiting for our official letter of confirmation from China. Our agency suggested that we not send anything until we received that. The thought of letting her birthday go by unnoticed saddened me, so we did send a package anyway. We had discovered that there was a Chinese woman living here in the States that had started a business sending care packages to children in China, most of whom were waiting in orphanages for their new families. We ordered the birthday care package that included a birthday cake, teddy bear, two disposable cameras in hopes the caretakers would take photos of Kaia, and a translated letter explaining the package and whom it was for. We wanted to send pictures of us but decided not to as we had not yet received the official acceptance letter from China. There was no guarantee that she would get the package, but we knew it was worth a try.

Care Packages

Sending a care package is a great way to make contact with your child before your arrival, especially if adopting an older child. You can include a letter, pictures of your family, toys, clothes, and disposable cameras. The pictures that are taken while your child is living in the orphanage or foster care will prove invaluable to your child as this may be the only glimpse of what life was like before they were adopted.

If interested in sending a care package, you may do it on your own; you will need the address of the orphanage and someone to translate the letter. However, if you prefer to have someone more experienced send your package, check out the following links.

www.blessedkids.com

www.redthreadchina.com

It was now July, and we expected another five- to six-month wait, but we received an unexpected phone call from our agency that we had received our letter of confirmation to adopt Kaia. This came much faster than expected. We had to sign the letter, send it back to China, then wait for the travel notice. It now looked like we would be travelling to China in two months! There were two other families from our agency that were going to adopt children from this orphanage, but only two of us received this notice. The third family didn't receive their confirmation until another several months had passed. There was no reason given; just another example of how unpredictable adoptions can be.

The first weekend of August is designated as "girls' weekend." For the past ten years or so, ten of my closest girlfriends from high school leave the husbands and kids home and spend a much-needed weekend away together. We usually rent a cabin on a lake in northern Michigan or stay at a nice resort, and this year was no different. It was late Friday morning, and we were almost at the lake when my cell phone rang. It was my secretary from the office and she said a woman called for me, but when she told her I was out of town, the woman said she'd just leave me a message at home. My secretary, knowing how important some of these adoption-related phone calls were, thought she recognized the voice as my adoption caseworker, and decided to let me know about this call.

I didn't think much about it at first because we didn't expect to hear anything from China for another three weeks. As I continued to drive, I started to get curious about the call. Kyle was working all day and wouldn't be home until late, and I couldn't call my answering machine at home because I never did set up a password to check messages remotely. I gave into curiosity and called the adoption agency. The call went through, but my cell phone coverage was horrible, and my phone hung up. I figured, *No big deal. We're almost to the cabin. I'll just call when I get to the lake.* Once we arrived, I walked out on the dock, where my reception was much better and tried the call again.

This time it went to the adoption agency's answering service as it was now just after noon, and they closed at noon on Fridays during the summer. What was it with these late Friday phone calls? I knew if the message was from our adoption consultant, she'd leave me an e-mail message in addition to the phone message, but unfortunately there was no Internet access at the cabin; this cabin didn't even have a television. Disappointed, I walked back up to the cabin and filled my friends in on my mystery phone call. I figured it would have to wait; after all it may not have had anything to do with the adoption anyway.

However, my friend Holly had a better idea. Before I knew it, she had her mom on the phone ready to hack into my e-mail. I gave her my e-mail address and password. She opened my e-mail and sure enough, there was a message from the adoption agency. As she read the message, I was in disbelief—the adoption agency had received our travel notice, and we were to leave for China in two weeks! We were expecting to have to wait at least another two months before traveling to China.

I asked her to repeat the message again. This time I repeated the message aloud as she read it to me. My group of friends erupted into screams of joy for us. What a way to start the weekend! It was like finding out I was pregnant with ten of my best friends to share in the excitement. After regaining composure, I ran back out on the dock and called Kyle at work. He too was shocked and speechless at first but just as excited as I. Our expected wait of six to nine months just turned into three and a half months! The next two weeks were a blur as we were busy planning and preparing.

International Travel Health

Depending on where you will be visiting, you may require additional immunizations or preventative medications. Consult your physician, a travel clinic, or go to www.cdc.gov for further recommendations.

We received our official itinerary shortly before traveling. We would leave Michigan on August 16, spend two days in Beijing sightseeing, and then fly to Ningxia province to get Kaia; we would spend approximately five days there processing paperwork. From there, we would fly to Guangzhou for our American embassy appointment and spend another five days there. Our boys were getting very excited to meet their new sister. They were only three- and five-years-old at the time, so we decided it would be better for them to stay home with family than to make the long trip to China, where chicken nuggets and macaroni and cheese might not always be readily available. It was difficult to think about being away from the boys that long, but they would be in good hands. Between my mom, Kyle's parents, and our siblings, we had it covered.

Figure 3: Map of China depicting our journey: 1) Beijing 2) Yinchuan 3) Guangzhou.

CHAPTER 5

China

∾ Day 1 ∾

We left our home the morning of August 16th. It was very difficult to say good-bye to the boys for two weeks, but they were excited for us to bring home their little sister. My grandparents took us to the local airport. We had a short flight to the Detroit airport, which went well. At the gate in Detroit we met our travel partner, Diane.

Diane was a single woman who was also adopting a little girl from Kaia's orphanage. Her daughter was three-years-old and had also been born with a cleft lip and palate, so we had something in common. Her daughter already had both the cleft lip and palate repaired and was fortunate enough to be living in foster care.

We were flying from Detroit to Tokyo to Beijing. We boarded the plane, and my notorious bad luck with flight delays struck. I'm not a frequent flier. I travel perhaps three times per year, but I seem to have the worst luck with flight delays or cancellations. I've spent more than one night in the Atlanta airport for weather-related delays, driven home from Chicago in a rental car because of a flight canceled by weather, had a drunk spill alcohol all over me and then pass out on my shoulder, been seated in the spot where the previous passenger had vomited—you get the idea. This time it was a battery charge failure that took an hour and twenty minutes to fix. This was going to give us only fifteen minutes to catch the next flight in Tokyo.

The passenger next to me was not having a very good flight as he continually got up to use the lavatory. Other than the smell of vomit that oozed from him, the flight went well. We landed in Tokyo and basically ran to our next flight, which they held for us. Seated around us on this flight were several Americans traveling to China to adopt just as we were. Two families were making their second adoption trip to China. There was a feeling of excitement from our fellow passengers that seemed contagious—after all we were all about to be parents.

We arrived in Beijing around 9:00 P.M. (China time). Our guide met us at the baggage claim area. Her name was Jane and she was very nice. A small bus took us to our hotel. By the time we arrived in our hotel room, twenty-seven hours had elapsed since we left our home in Michigan. To say we were exhausted was an understatement. We wanted and needed to sleep, but it was so exciting to finally be in

China. We stayed at the River View Hotel, and it was very nice. The only major difference from the hotel there and one here in the United States was that the mattresses were very hard. It felt more like we were sleeping on the floor than the bed.

∽ Day 2 ∽

We were only able to sleep until 4:00 A.M. because of excitement and the twelve-hour time difference. That morning we went down to breakfast, which thoroughly impressed Kyle. The Chinese are serious about their breakfast buffets. The amount of food was overwhelming. I think Kyle tried some of everything despite the fact that he had no idea what most of it was. I was not quite as adventuresome right away.

We then met another adoptive couple who would be traveling with us. They were a very nice couple from Colorado—Tim and Kristen. Kristen was deaf, but did an amazing job of reading lips. They were adopting a boy with a hearing impairment. Their son was living in a different province than we would be traveling, but they would be with us in Beijing and Guangzhou.

That morning Jane met up with us for a full day of sightseeing. The weather was humid and hot—mid-90s. Our first stop was Tiananmen Square and the Forbidden

City. Our guide was great at educating us on Chinese history, but it was hard to concentrate because there were so many people there. We were shoulder to shoulder with other hot, sweaty tourists. I was salivating for ice-cold water. Bottled water was available for purchase, but it was always room temperature. Because of the large population in Beijing, demands on electricity were often more than could be delivered, thus luxuries such as refrigerated water were hard to find.

I can honestly say I've never seen so many people in one place as when we toured the Forbidden City. The architecture of the buildings was amazing, but the crowds were distracting. For lunch, our guide took us to an authentic Chinese restaurant, so we could get a real taste of China. This restaurant was popular with the locals. We were seated in our own private room upstairs. The place was loud and the thing I noticed first was the number of young children working in the restaurant. Our guide told us that not all children have the same opportunities for an education and thus start working at a fairly young age.

Our guide ordered a variety of food for us. We had a major feast, and it only cost $8/person. This was also our first experience with restrooms without a Western-style toilet. Many businesses and airports have what is commonly referred to as a squat toilet—it's more of a squat and pee in the hole. This was the first of many squat toilets; most had a curtain for privacy but not all had a sink.

After lunch we walked around the downtown area off the beaten tourist path. There we were able to see traditional housing and small family-owned businesses. Beijing is known for its pearls, so we also went to a pearl factory. We learned a lot about pearls and were informed that the next day was Valentine's Day in China. Of course we had to buy a string of pearls then! From there, we went to The Heavenly Garden and saw the well-known Temple of Heaven. Again the architecture and attention to detail is amazing. It's a very large building made of twenty-eight piers, three stories tall, and no nails holding it together. If you've ever been to Epcot Center in Orlando, when you enter the land of China, this is the building they have replicated there.

By now we were not only hot, but exhausted, too. Kyle bought a Popsicle from a vendor in green bean flavor, which apparently is a local favorite. Did I mention Kyle would try anything once? We then went back to our hotel rooms long enough to change. Jane had plans for us to go to an acrobatics show. It was nice to sit, and we enjoyed the show, but we were exhausted. Again we thought it was amazing how young some of these performers were, yet already so precise and perfect in their movements. These children were trained from a very young age.

After this very busy day, we couldn't wait to get back to our rooms and sleep. I unfortunately started feeling poorly that day. My head ached, I was congested, and my nose wouldn't stop running. It felt like a sinus infection, but I later learned it was the smog that was making me feel that way. Beijing is a city of approximately 15 million, and it was preparing to host the 2008 Summer Olympics. In order to decrease the amount of traffic and pollution, they had just started restricting the amount of cars on the roads the day before our arrival. For instance, if it was an even day, only cars with license plates ending in an even number could be on the roads that day. Everyone was commenting on how much less traffic there was, but I'm here to tell you that it was still very busy. The streets were packed, and it wasn't uncommon to have three lanes of vehicles on a two-lane road. Many people commute by bicycle and on foot.

It didn't take long to figure out that pedestrians do not have the right of way in China as they do here in the United States. Once you step off the curb it's every man for himself. We noticed several women wearing large hats or white veils that covered their faces. I asked our guide about this, and she told me that young Chinese women want their skin to be light colored and protect their skin from the sun. Makeup in China is marketed for keeping skin light. Ironically, light-skinned women in the United States spend lots of money at tanning salons and buy tanning lotions to darken the skin. I guess it's another classic example of wanting what you can't have.

Figure 4: The author and her husband enjoying a traditional Chinese meal.

∽ Day 3 ∽

Once again, we woke early and headed down to the large breakfast buffet. After Kyle had sampled just about everything, we met up with our group to see the Great Wall. The area we were to visit was an hour and a half out of town. On the way, we stopped at a jade factory, where we received yet another education, this time about jade. I'm pretty sure the salespeople look forward to American tourists because they know most of us will do our share to help their local economy. They told us it was a Chinese tradition for a mother to hand down jade to her daughter on her wedding day.

After spending some money there, we were off to eat. The restaurant was situated in a valley and when we looked up at the mountain, we got our first glimpse of the Great Wall. This restaurant was a bit more touristy, but there was excellent food once again. I was very excited to walk on the Great Wall, and I can honestly say it was nothing like I had expected. It was much more spectacular than I had imagined. The first thing that struck me was this huge wall was located at the top of a mountain. We had to ride up the mountain in a sky trolley car that was similar to what we have at ski resorts. Apparently we were at a frequently visited area of the wall as our guide told us that Bill Clinton came to this same place when he visited China during his presidency. She spoke very highly of him, and she said he was instrumental in improving relations between China and the United States.

The side of the mountain was covered in vegetation and trees. The ride up was miserable as the trolley car was enclosed, and it was again humid and in the mid-90s. Once we reached the top, it was all worth it. The air was clean, and without the smog, my congestion was gone. After a bit more walking uphill, we finally reached the wall. We all went our separate ways and walked on the wall. There were watchtowers that provided much-needed shade. This part of the wall was in excellent condition. It stretched as far as your eyes could see in both directions; only the fog limited the view.

As we stood there gazing out, we were absolutely awestruck to be standing on this structure that extends 5,000 kilometers and took more than two millennia to be completed by manpower alone. This place is a true example that with enough hard work and determination, you can accomplish anything. A famous Chinese saying is, "One who fails to reach the Great Wall would not be regarded as a hero." Even standing on this great wonder of the world couldn't make me forget the real reason for this visit—tomorrow we would get our daughter. The sightseeing was great, but the entire time I was counting down the hours until I would meet my little girl.

Figure 5: The author and her husband on the Great Wall.

After we came down from the wall, many sellers met us. They were selling everything from T-shirts to artwork. Many of the people had similar items. It gave us a chance to work on our bartering skills. It was not uncommon for a T-shirt to start out at 150 yuan, but you could actually buy it for 50 yuan and sometimes less. (One hundred yuan equaled about fourteen U.S. dollars.) I bought a silk dress for Kaia, some T-shirts, and a painted scroll.

It was now mid-afternoon, and we headed back into the city. We all had flights out of Beijing that night. Our flight was to depart to Ningxia that night at 8:00. We had done a lot of walking that day, so our guide wanted to treat us with a foot massage before going to the airport. It was a ninety-minute "foot" massage that included the feet, legs, back, shoulders, arms, etc. We all sat in one room side by side for our massages. The women who did the massages worked in sync with each other and the sounds of their hands made a wonderfully rhythmic sound. The massage was excellent but downright painful at times. These young, beautiful, petite women were nearly bringing tears to two grown men's eyes with the pounding of their hands. Kyle is still amazed at their strength. It was by far the best, and most beautiful sounding, massage I'll probably ever have.

From there, we went straight to the airport. Saying good-bye to Jane was bittersweet. We had only known her for two days, but it was sad to leave because she had become our friend. She had made us feel safe in this big city. It was at this point in our journey that our group split up. Tim and

Kristen were on a flight to Kunming, where their son was living, and Diane would continue on with us to Ningxia. Both Kaia and Diane's daughter, Zoe, were living in the same orphanage. Diane's daughter had been living with a foster family, but we were told that the children are usually brought back to the orphanage a few days before the adoption day.

As we sat in the airport waiting for our flight to Ningxia, I noticed I was one of only a handful of women about to board this flight. The remaining passengers were men in business suits carrying briefcases. They called for our flight, and we walked through the gate into the darkness outside to find a bus that would take us to our plane. Everyone boarded the bus, and we were crammed in like a herd of cattle. There were not nearly enough seats, so we stood and did our best not to fall into the next person pressed against us. After a short ride, the bus stopped in front of a plane. It was a shoving match to see who could get off the bus the fastest. It was dark out, and the area was poorly lit. As we walked up the stairs to board the plane, I was right behind Kyle. By the time Kyle reached the top, I was still near the bottom of the stairs as I was repeatedly pushed out of the way. The men seemed to treat me with complete disregard. If that happened here in the States, I probably would have yelled out a sarcastic, "Excuse you!" But the fact of the matter was I was the foreigner in their country. I could not speak the language, and I needed to play by their rules now. It was clear to me that women were not on the same playing field as the men. Kyle and I were seated in the very last row, so our seats would not recline. It was a turbulent flight that lasted about one and a half hours. I was utterly exhausted and managed to sleep for a few minutes on the flight.

Once we landed, the three of us found our luggage and headed out of the airport, where our guide, Frank, was waiting for us. The airport was small, and the only people in the airport were from our flight. On the bus to the hotel, Frank told us that there were approximately 200 children in this orphanage and confirmed what we already knew, that very few international adoptions take place there. I asked about Kaia, and he said that he spoke with the orphanage. They said she was cute and small but did not talk much. He told us both Kaia and Zoe were healthy. We arrived at the Ningxia International Hotel, and Frank checked us in. It was now late. I posted an update and photos of our day on an online journal that we used to keep in touch with family and friends. Kyle wrote in his journal, and we were off to sleep—mere hours before we would meet Kaia. Frank would meet us in the hotel lobby at 8:40 A.M. to go get our daughters.

◌ Day 4 ◌

Gotcha Day! We woke at 6:30 that morning, with butterflies in our stomachs. We prepared the necessary paperwork—there was a lot we needed that day. We also brought gifts such as chocolates and lotions for the orphanage director, caretakers, and notary officials. We went down to breakfast to find the buffet breakfast was even larger than the buffet in the previous hotel. Kyle had several plates, but I only had one because I was too excited to eat. Emotions were running high that morning. I was a combination of excitement, anxiety, and fear all rolled into one.

At the scheduled time, Frank met Kyle, me, and Diane in the hotel lobby. He checked to make sure we had the required paperwork with us. It was a short five-minute bus ride from the hotel. We pulled up to the orphanage. It was in the middle of a city block. From the street, it looked like a three-story white building. There was a gated entrance, which was opened for us after Frank spoke with the man at the gate. We walked in through a courtyard. There were a few older boys standing there as we walked by. The boys stopped what they were doing and stared at us with a look of confusion on their faces. It was obvious the orphanage was much bigger than it appeared from the street. We were ushered into the building, and I recognized a mural on the wall that other adoptive families had their pictures taken in front of.

We were taken to the first room on the right. It was a nicely decorated conference room with a large wooden table down the center of the room. The walls were painted a warm green, and there were a few artificial flowers used to decorate the room. There we met the orphanage director. She was a pretty woman with two stacks of documents in front of her—one for us and the other for Diane. There were brief introductions and then she thanked us for adopting the girls and providing them a family. She presented to both Diane and me a white sheep's hair scarf that was locally made. It was a very unexpected gesture that I will always treasure. Next we started signing official documents stating we would never abandon, abuse, or neglect our daughter. She then gave us a small photo of Kaia that was to be used for her passport. We were told it was taken two days earlier.

When I first glanced at the photo, a wave of terror swept over me. It didn't look like our daughter. She was dressed in boy's clothes, her hair was shaved close to her head, and she was standing. I'd only seen her referral photos and one updated photo that were all taken several months before. I looked at Kyle with what I'm sure was a very concerned look and whispered, "Is that her?" He nodded yes with a very reassuring look as if to say "Look closely." I did look closely, and yes, that was our daughter; she had just grown up a lot since those last photos.

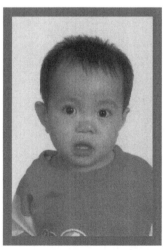

The paperwork only took five to ten minutes, and then the director called for the girls. My heart was racing, and I had a nauseous feeling in my stomach as we waited for them to arrive. Just a mere moment later, the door opened, and there they were! As soon as I saw Kaia there was no question in my mind— this was our daughter. This is the

Figure 6: Kaia's passport photograph.

little girl in the photos that I'd been staring at and dreaming about for the past three and a half months. Feelings of joy swept over me.

There was a nanny with each girl. The nannies walked in holding the little girls' hands. As soon as our new daughters saw us they both started crying. Kaia clung to the nanny who was now holding her. I tried to talk to Kaia as the nanny was still holding her. I had brought a small doll and tried to give that to her, but she continued to cry. The look on her face told me she was fearful of this man and woman that looked and sounded so different. I started to cry for her, too. She started to calm down after a couple of minutes.

The orphanage director wanted the girls to go to the mothers, so Kyle stepped back to capture some photographs of this momentous occasion. (We were not allowed to bring in a video camera.) After five minutes of this brief introduction, the director instructed the nannies to give the girls to us. I was finally holding my daughter! It was bittersweet, as she started crying again. The nanny tried to comfort Kaia as I held her, and she did finally stop crying. Diane's daughter, Zoe, unfortunately didn't settle down and continued to cry vehemently.

The director informed us, "You must go now." They marched us out of the orphanage as quickly as possible. At one point someone put a hand on my back as if to say "Move along, please." We didn't get to stop for a photo by the wall as other families had done, and when Kyle lifted the camera to take a picture of Kaia and me, they told him, "No take picture of crying baby." As we left, we were given a small box that had the contents of her birthday care package that we had sent two months earlier: a teddy bear and two disposable cameras, which were used but undeveloped. Our daughter had lived in that orphanage all of her life, and yet she left there with only the clothes on her back and the care package we had sent. We sat back on the bus, this time with our daughter on my lap. I remember looking at Kyle and saying, "What just happened?" The whole experience was only twenty minutes long at the most. We were not allowed to ask any questions, tour the orphanage, etc. It was probably one of the oddest situations I have ever experienced.

Our guide and one of the nannies from the orphanage came along on the bus to help with the girls. Zoe was still crying, and the nanny did her best to calm her. I used this opportunity to ask questions about what Kaia ate or her sleep patterns, etc., but the answers were always very brief. Kaia sat on my lap motionless as if she was in shock. It was at that moment that I realized she was burning up with a fever. Shortly after that, she started coughing. It was the kind of wet-sounding cough that makes everyone look and say "Aww, poor baby."

I had brought medications with me, but we had official paperwork to sign before going back to the hotel. After a very short bus ride, we were at a small photo lab to have a family photo taken. This is the photo that would be used for the adoption paperwork. Following that we were back on the bus to the civil affairs office, where the adoption was completed. The orphanage director and the civil affairs agent met us. We had to sign more paperwork and once again swear not to harm or abandon her. They needed a handprint from Kaia, which made the crying start all over again, and Kyle and I inked our thumbprints over our signatures. We were there for what seemed like hours, most of it just sitting and waiting in the unbearable heat.

As we sat there, Kaia started coughing again. The civil affairs woman looked at Kaia concerned and then turned to the orphanage director and started speaking in Chinese while looking at Kaia. Kyle asked our guide what they were talking about and his response was, "Nothing." Obviously, we didn't believe him. I may not speak Chinese, but body language is a universal language, and to this day, I am sure they were talking about Kaia's sickness. Maybe many children were sick and that's why we were sent out so fast, I'll never know. I guess the thing that made me the most irritated was that they knew Kaia was sick but ignored it and continued to tell us she was fine. Our guide also ignored the fact that she had a fever and cough, but I remained quiet. Again, I was in their country, and they were allowing me to adopt this beautiful child. I had dealt with sick children before; I just couldn't wait to get back to the hotel to check her over and start her on antibiotics and a fever reducer.

A while later, the nanny showed me how to take Kaia to the bathroom. Most children and caretakers in China do not have the luxury of diapers, so the children wear split pants. It's exactly what it sounds like; the pants are split, so they can easily go potty. We took her to the restroom, and she picked Kaia up in the sitting position and held her over the hole. Apparently, the children were taken to potty on a routine. I had to wonder how many "accidents" they encountered in a day. Kaia did not go, but I attributed it to the state of shock she was in. It was very hot, and I was concerned about dehydration, but they didn't send anything with her to drink out of. We tried to give her water from a cup, but it was very evident that she'd never used a cup as it spilled all over her, and she just choked on it.

Zoe was now doing much better and warming up to Diane. They were even blowing kisses back and forth. Zoe was a very cute little girl. She was in foster care, and looked and acted very differently from Kaia. She'd also already had her cleft lip and palate repaired and was thus able to speak and drink out of a cup. Zoe had a very dark tan and longer hair in four pigtails. Kaia was pale and her hair was shaved close to her head, I assume to help prevent lice in the orphanage. After what seemed like an eternity, the paperwork was finally complete. We presented a gift of chocolate to the civil affairs woman, and we got back on the bus to go back to the hotel.

Medications: What to bring?

An entire chapter could be devoted to travel medicine, but keep in mind there are a few medications that you may want to bring for both yourself and your child. For your child:

- Antibiotic: something effective for ear infections and upper respiratory tract infections (in powder form).
- Scabies medication
- Lice treatment
- Acetaminophen or Ibuprofen (age appropriate)
- Antihistamine (Benadryl)
- Diaper rash cream
- Lotion: Aquaphor is a good choice
- Glycerin suppositories
- Thermometer
- Medicine dropper
- Triple antibiotic ointment and Band-Aids

For adults

- Antibiotic in case of traveler's diarrhea
- Antidiarrheal such as Imodium
- Acetaminophen or Ibuprofen

For prescription medications, you will need to discuss this with your physician/pediatrician. Not all physicians will be comfortable prescribing medications "just in case." Remember to keep all medications in their original containers.

Upon returning to our hotel room, I took out the medical supplies that I had brought and examined Kaia. As a PA, I couldn't wait any longer to help this obviously sick little girl and examine her from head to toe. I felt like a mom of a newborn baby—checking to make sure the baby had all her fingers and toes. Upon examining her cleft palate I saw that it was large—larger than I had expected. The cleft palate was about 1–2cm wide from her top teeth all the way to the back of her throat. Her top teeth were anything but straight. Her fever was 102.3 degrees F, and her lung sounds were consistent with pneumonia. In fact, she had probably some of the worst sounding lungs I've ever heard.

I'd brought antibiotics and Ibuprofen, which we started right then and there. She weighed a mere twenty pounds, and her muscle tone was poor. We were able to get her to drink a small amount of water from a bottle that I had brought and even a bite or two of soft foods. She lay down and took a nap without a cry. We sat on the bed watching her sleep as she sucked her thumb. As with all new parents, we took pictures of her while she slept. She was beautiful. It was hard to believe, she was finally ours.

Our quiet family time was short-lived, as our guide picked us up at 2:30 P.M. to take us to the bank to exchange money. At the time of our adoption, the required orphanage donation was $3,000. We were told they wanted it in crisp $100 bills, but this orphanage wanted it in RMB, which is the local currency. We went to a large bank where they exchanged our American money for RMB, and then had to walk about one and a half blocks to another bank to deposit it in the orphanage's account. Earlier in the day, our guide told us to beware of pick-pockets, so Kyle was a bit nervous walking with such a big wad of cash in his pocket. Thankfully, everything went well.

From there we walked to the notary office to sign more of the same paperwork we had already signed twice earlier in the day. As we walked in the streets of Ningxia, we were a spectacle. People came out of their stores to stare at us as we walked by. Yinchuan is not an area frequented by tourists, and we were possibly the first foreigners that some of these people had ever seen. Remember, international adoptions were not common at this orphanage, so we were an oddity. Kyle has red hair, so I think that was also a point of conversation for many Chinese. They appeared so confused as to why these Americans were carrying a Chinese baby. I was getting exhausted; it was hot, and Kaia was starting to get heavy. She preferred me to hold her over Kyle, which we were prepared for. Most of the reading and researching about adopting from China that we did before our trip indicated that the girls were often fearful of men and attached to females more readily; Kaia was no exception. The notary office was hot, and the air heavy. Kaia sat on my lap completely lethargic. She never made a sound the whole time we were there. After our paperwork was complete at the notary office, we gave the young woman there a gift of chocolates, and we were back on the bus to the hotel.

Once in our room, it was apparent that the Ibuprofen was working as her fever was much less, and she seemed more alert. We tried to get her to walk, but she was very unsteady on her own. She was able to walk with finger assistance. She did walk to Kyle and let him give her a hug, which was exactly what he needed. I tried to take her potty, but not being used to a Western-style toilet, she was afraid of it and didn't seem to understand it was okay to go potty in this thing. We put her in a pull-up diaper that we'd brought from home. She was only twenty-six-months-old and going through a lot of changes; potty training was the least of my worries.

Before I traveled to China, I thought one of the first things I would do with my daughter is give her a bath and change her clothes. Somehow, that changed. I was in no hurry to traumatize her any more than we already had. All of a sudden Kaia started crying loudly like she was scared or hurt. I realized she had just wet her diaper. She cried inconsolably while I changed her diaper. We have to wonder if the children were scolded when they had an accident based on this experience. You couldn't help but feel bad for her. She finally calmed down and sat still while I tried to engage her to play, but mostly she just watched me act like a lunatic trying to make her smile. Again, she sat there quietly.

We needed more diapers and milk, so Kyle went to a small market just a half block from the hotel that our guide had told us about. Unfortunately, the store was closed when Kyle got there, but while he was gone, something miraculous happened—Kaia smiled! She and

I were sitting on the bed, and I was trying to be funny again, and then it happened. She smiled. I was pretending to drink from her bottle and every time I made loud gulping sounds she smiled. I was elated! This is the first time she really interacted with me, and I was even able to sneak a picture of her smiling. I wished Kyle were there to see it, but once he got back, she wouldn't smile anymore. I assumed it was because she wasn't feeling well, but I later realized she quit smiling because Kyle was back in the room. She was far more comfortable with me than Kyle. Her only experience with men was probably at medical appointments, and I'm sure these were traumatic.

Later on she got very fussy again. I took her to the bathroom to try and go potty, but that's not what she wanted. For the first time, she was assertive and took my finger and walked to the door and banged on it. She wanted us to take her back. We had taken her from the only home she'd ever known and she wanted to go back. By now I was crying too. It was heartbreaking. In our pre-adoption education, they had warned us about these things, but nothing can prepare you for it when your child is so scared.

It was dinnertime, so we did our best to console her and occupy her with food. We ordered room service, but she only ate one mouthful of noodles and spit every other thing out. She did eat some leftover cold French fries, and we were able to get her to drink three ounces of warm milk once we cut the nipple large enough. With her cleft palate, she had troubles sucking, so she chewed on the nipple. I brought a variety of bottles and nipples in anticipation of her cleft palate, but none of them seemed to work. With her fever, I was very concerned about dehydration and actually used the syringe from the Ibuprofen to feed her some milk. The next day I planned to ask our guide to contact the orphanage for a bottle that she was used to drinking out of. I knew it would be a long shot but worth a try. At that point, I would have paid $100 for one bottle that she would drink from. That night we laid her down on the bed and lay next to her. She stuck her thumb in her mouth and went right to sleep without a cry.

We had made it through our first day, and it was an emotional rollercoaster. I posted photos and the day's events on our blog, and Kyle wrote in his journal, and then we crashed hard, too.

Figure 7: Mother and daughter minutes after being united together.

∽ Day 5 ∽

We had a great night. Other than stirring when she coughed, Kaia slept from 9:00 P.M. to 7:00 A.M. She woke up with a high fever again. We gave her more Ibuprofen and about an hour later, she started feeling better. We ordered some warm milk in hopes that she would drink today. We put it in the same bottle that we had offered her the night before, and to our surprise she chugged the whole bottle down! The little stinker could suck out of our bottle just fine! We couldn't have been happier.

I then washed her in the sink. Our hotel room only had a shower stall, which I thought would have scared her, so we went with a bath in the sink. She didn't mind it. We dressed her in a cute little green skirt and matching shirt. She was adorable. We introduced her to some toys that we had brought from home. She did show some interest in them. She sat on the floor and rolled the ball back and forth to Kyle for a few minutes. As long as he was a few feet away from her she was fine but got very anxious when he tried to pick her up or hug her.

As I watched her play, I noticed that she would take all of the balls and put them in one place then move them to another over and over again. She was almost neurotic in the way she moved her toys. She was able to walk around the hotel room on her own but was very unsteady. Once she fell down, she was unable to crawl or stand back up. I got on all fours trying to show her how to crawl, but it was obvious that she'd never crawled before. As you know with any young child learning to walk, they fall down all the time but are able to crawl or pull themselves back up. Kaia couldn't do that. Once she fell, she was stuck in that spot like a turtle on its back. It was heartbreaking, but that just told me we'd be playing on the floor a lot to develop those muscles and skills.

We went to the hotel breakfast buffet, and Kaia did very well eating. She was very hesitant to feed herself. She was hungry but just stared at her food. It was evident that she'd never fed herself. I started feeding her, and she ate very well. I made her a plate of food and put it in front of her. After much encouragement, she started to feed herself. With the cleft palate, we could only feed her soft foods, but that didn't seem to be a problem as there were multiple pastries and fruits. Her favorite was congee, which is a combination of rice and milk served warm. I believe this was very familiar to her from the orphanage. Zoe, who was only eleven months older than Kaia, was completely independent when it came to eating. This was just one of the many differences we would discover about the development for a child living in a foster care home compared to an orphanage. After breakfast we hung out in our room, and Kaia went down for a nap at 11:00 A.M.

Three hours later, Kaia awoke, again with a fever. We were basically giving her Ibuprofen every eight hours to keep the fever down and keep her feeling better. Later that afternoon, our guide met us and took us to a large department store to buy supplies. It was about eight blocks from the hotel. The shopping area was very large, and it reminded me of a large Macy's or Younkers. We bought Kaia a pair of shoes and some diapers. Diane bought a stroller for Zoe. After we made our purchases in the department store, our guide took us to the basement, and there was a huge grocery store there. I found Pampers diapers, but didn't buy them because we'd already bought diapers upstairs and suitcase space and weight were precious. (Domestic flights within China had a maximum baggage weight of only forty-four pounds.) They even had Heinz baby food. It was expensive at $1.00 for a small bottle. Our guide had never heard of it, and I'm pretty sure he thought I was crazy when I bought it. It seemed perfect to me because it was soft, and I could keep it in the hotel room with me. As it turned out, I *was* crazy for buying it because Kaia refused to eat any of it the entire trip.

We also bought some Coke, bottled water, snacks, and milk in pint containers that needed no refrigeration for Kaia. Before arriving at the department store, we dropped off our disposable cameras at the camera shop. When we stopped back after shopping, the photos were done. The female workers remembered us and were very excited to talk to the girls. For a small fee, they enlarged our adoption picture that they had taken the day before, so we'd have our own copy. We were then taken back to the hotel, and our guide informed us he would be back in two days to pick us up and do more paperwork. Kyle questioned him about this, and he informed us that he has another job that he had to attend to. He suggested that we just stay in the hotel. It was clear that he was there only to facilitate the adoption paperwork and appointments. He did seem very knowledgeable in the entire process but had no desire to show us around the city. I guess I shouldn't have been too disappointed as Kaia was much too ill to be out on sightseeing trips anyway.

That night we went to the familiar hotel buffet for dinner with Diane and Zoe. There was a massive amount of food to choose from. Both girls ate very well, which was again a sigh of relief. The food in our hotel was much more expensive when compared to other restaurants that we'd eaten at since arriving in China. Our bill for two buffet dinners came to $38. Before I knew it we were back to the room again to play. Kaia drank a quarter of the bottle of congee before going to bed. Although that day had gone very well, I couldn't help but notice that Kaia still had not attempted to make a sound other than crying. She never once babbled or cooed. Other than crying, she was silent.

Once she was sound asleep we looked at the pictures that we had developed. These were from the two disposable cameras sent in our care package. We didn't even know if they would use them, and we weren't sure what to expect. However, after only seeing the first few photos I knew this was one of the best things we did thus far. The caretakers did an excellent job of taking pictures of our little girl. They included pictures of her eating, in her crib, playing with other children, and posed in many of the areas within the orphanage. They used every picture on both cameras. Someday these photos will surely be priceless to Kaia as this will be her only glimpse of her life in China. Having these photos was worth every penny it cost to send the care package, and I would recommend it to any adoptive family.

∾ Day 6 ∾

The night went pretty well, and Kaia's fever wasn't as high that morning as it had been during the previous days. We gave her medicine and a bottle of warm milk. I was ready for a shower, but Kaia was afraid if I was out of her eyesight. Kyle tried to keep her happy, but she still was unsure of what to think of Kyle. I remembered that I brought along a Baby Einstein DVD that the boys loved so much when they were little, so I popped it in the laptop. Much to our surprise, she was mesmerized by it and sat on Kyle's lap as she watched the movie. I took my shower and as I was drying off, I heard the most beautiful sound— Kaia was making sounds at the movie! I threw open the bathroom door to see a very excited little girl totally engaged and pointing at the movie, and her dad sitting there smiling. Thank you, God! She was attempting to speak! This was a momentous occasion in my eyes. I was thrilled, but Kyle was elated. The wall between Kaia and Kyle was slowly coming down. She sat on his lap nearly thirty minutes that morning—a huge breakthrough for daddy and daughter.

After getting dressed, we were off for yet another hotel breakfast. Kaia ate fairly well, but we were getting stir-crazy sitting in the hotel all day. We had learned that there was a park in the middle of the city, and Kyle called our guide to ask about going there. He told us that he was too busy to take us, but he did speak with the hotel attendant who helped us a little. The attendant wrote down the name of the park in Chinese on the back of the hotel business card so that all we had to do was show the taxi driver the handwritten side of the card to go to the park, and the printed side of the card when we wanted to come back to the hotel.

Kaia was ready for a nap before we were to venture out. After another three-hour nap, she woke with yet another fever. I gave her more Ibuprofen, but she was now becoming an expert at spitting it out. Giving her the antibiotic and Ibuprofen became more of a challenge, but one that I always won, nonetheless. Once she started feeling better, we headed off on our outing. The hotel business card worked great. We showed it to the bellboy, who smiled and hailed us a cab. He told the driver where to take us. We felt pretty stupid when we arrived at the park about three or four blocks away from the hotel. We could have easily walked there.

The park was located along the street, and there was a large open gate at the entrance. We were unsure if we needed to pay to get in, but the attendant waved us in. The park was beautiful. It was the first grass I'd seen since arriving in Yinchuan. There were beautiful flowers and tall trees. Several large ponds were connected together. Many local men were fishing with long cane poles. We did see someone catch a small fish. The water was very brown, and it was difficult to tell how deep the water was. They had paddleboats and electric boats available for rent. One end of the park had carnival rides, and there was even a small zoo within the park.

We stopped to rest and sit in the lush green grass. I sat Kaia down in the grass, and she became upset and scared. We reassured her that it was okay. I lay in the grass and rolled around all the while laughing, so that she knew this poky green stuff was okay. We took some pictures and sat there for a while enjoying the park. A man sat down about fifteen yards from us and stared at us. I thought he was going to ask for money. He never said anything to us; he just stared.

Then, in an instant, Kaia started feeling poorly again and was running another fever. She wanted to be held. It was very hot, and she didn't feel well, so we opted to head back even though we'd only been there for a short time. My arms ached as I carried her. It got to the point that I couldn't carry her any longer, so Kyle had to carry her. She didn't throw a fit when he took her, but I don't think she had the energy to object.

I couldn't help but to feel awkward the entire time we were in the park. Everyone stared at us. As we were walking back on the trail, a man on a bike passed us going the same way. He turned around and gawked at us so hard his bike went off the trail and nearly crashed. I felt somewhat uneasy walking around town without our guide. I was fearful that we'd be questioned as to why we had this Chinese child. Would they think we were abducting her? Fortunately, no one questioned us, but by the time we made it to the park entrance, we were all so hot and miserable that we knew for sure we'd get a cab back. We jumped in a cab that was waiting on the street and showed him the hotel card. He stared at us in his rearview mirror, and when we spoke to each other in English he laughed. As we came to a red light, he turned around and stared at Kaia and me until the light turned green. I have to wonder what he was thinking. Regardless, we made it back to the hotel without any issues.

The rest of the day, Kaia decided that she wanted *nothing* to do with Kyle. If Kyle even went near her, she would whine and cry, and hold her arms out toward me. She acted like Kyle was the meanest person on earth, and it tore me to pieces. Although Kyle tried to act like it didn't bother him, I knew it was tearing him apart. Little did this little girl know, she had one of the best dads on earth right in front of her. We went down for dinner, and things went from bad to worse. We ordered pizza Americana as we thought a taste of home would be a nice change. We didn't get to enjoy it because Kaia turned into the true meaning of the terrible twos. She threw everything she could get her hands on, whether it was food, silverware, or a table decoration. A little boy from a nearby table came over to pick up the things she threw. We did find out that Kaia is left-handed with all the throwing that night. If we told her no, she screamed and threw more.

After an embarrassing night at the hotel dining room, we went back to our room. Kaia was clearly agitated now, and crying and carrying on. We then noticed she was holding her butt. We attributed it to constipation as she hadn't had a bowel movement since we got her two days earlier, likely due to her change in diet. She finally had a hard bowel movement before going to bed that night, but it was small, and she still seemed uncomfortable. She fell asleep, but woke up crying every thirty minutes. It was a very emotional day and night. I sat on the end of the bed exhausted. I started crying; what had we gotten ourselves into? This was not easy. Our daughter wanted nothing to do with Kyle, she was angry and acting out, not to mention still very sick. Would things ever get better? I didn't have a positive thing to say about the day. I couldn't bring myself to make an entry into the online journal that night, so Kyle took over for me. We had so many friends and family at home looking forward to daily updates; we hated to let them down.

∾ Day 7 ∾

We had a horrible night. The "pizza Americana" didn't fare well with my GI tract, and Kaia woke up crying repeatedly throughout the night. She also wet right through her diaper. The department store diapers that we bought didn't have fasteners (and we had no tape in the room) so we used a pull-up over top of the diaper thinking it might hold it in place. As luck would have it, there was zero absorbency to the diapers we bought, and the pull-up did not stay in place. The only good thing about the situation was we didn't have to do the laundry. I had attributed the multiple crying spells in the night to constipation so I gave Kaia a suppository. About thirty minutes later, we were ever so happy to see a diaper full of poo, or as Kyle so eloquently put it, "A pile of boulders that would have made a grown man cry." I do admit our little girl did seem happier after that major event. This was also the first morning that she didn't wake with a fever.

We then went about our normal routine and went downstairs to the hotel breakfast. Meanwhile, Diane was having some issues with paperwork, so she called our adoption agency back in the States for their help. While she was on the phone with them, she complained about our guide. It was true he was trying to get by doing the bare minimum, and he was opinionated and chauvinistic, but he was facilitating the adoption paperwork with ease nonetheless. Apparently after that phone call, her consultant contacted the Chinese coordinator, who then called our guide. We had no idea this was taking place until a hotel staff member came up to me while we were eating breakfast to tell me I had a phone call.

I went to the phone, and it was Frank. He asked if I wanted him to take us to the local hospital so that a doctor could evaluate Kaia for her cold. I was speechless! This is the same man that had refused to acknowledge that Kaia was sick. The first two days he would ask how the girls were doing, and I told him that Kaia was very sick and running a fever, but his response was always, "She okay." Without hesitation, I told him, "No, thank you." I had made it this long, I wasn't about to take her to a hospital there and lose control of the situation and likely postpone our departure from Yinchuan. We were to leave Yinchuan the next day and fly to Guangzhou, where there were many Western-trained doctors who could see her if she got worse. I came right out and asked him why he was offering now, and he responded that Diane complained about him to his boss, and he was very upset about this. It was clear that he was going to try to keep us happy the next day and a half until we left.

After breakfast we went back to the room to play with Kaia. She was a little better around Kyle this day, but she still would not allow him to touch her or pick her up. The fact that he could be in the same room as her was a huge improvement from the night before. I was sitting on a chair and had Kaia on my lap facing me. We were playing with a ball when all of a sudden she leaned over and bit my breast so hard that I screamed out in surprise and pain. She responded by laughing. This was the first time we heard her laugh, and it was the most inappropriate of times. I took her off my lap and sat her on the floor next to me and said in a very firm voice, "No no!" I acted very sad and hurt, but she didn't seem to care in the least. After a short period of time I got on the floor to play with her and the same thing happened. Out of the blue she slapped me across the cheek and smiled. My emotions at that time are beyond words. Was she trying to punish me for taking her from her home and friends? Or, was she so socially challenged that she thought this was okay? Thankfully, Kaia settled down for her late morning nap because by now I was a sleep-deprived emotional mess. I lay down for a nap too, and Kyle ventured out to find new diapers. The following is the entry that Kyle posted on our journal:

"Marie was tired, so she hung out with Kaia, and I went on a mission to find some more diapers that hopefully work and have adhesive straps on them. Pull-ups are nowhere to be found in China. I walked about a mile down the road looking in a few shops. These shops are a lot different than stores back home. They literally are small, specialized stores about twelve feet wide by twenty feet deep with usually only one person in them. I finally found a corner store that reminded me of a party store, with a little bit of everything. I looked around for a bit then had to go ask for help. Now imagine a red-headed Caucasian guy who doesn't speak a lick of Chinese trying to describe diapers to four Chinese ladies who don't speak a lick of English. I tried to get the baby idea across, and they just looked confused. Then a lady with a little boy came in. I pointed at him and then formed a diaper in my crotch with my hands and pointed back to the little boy. They knew exactly what I wanted and took me directly to the diapers. They also proceeded to laugh the rest of the time I was in the store. Ten diapers *with* adhesive tape for $2.50— mission complete."

Later that afternoon, Frank picked us up to have more paperwork notarized. Our travel partner Diane had more issues with the paperwork, so what was supposed to take thirty minutes ended up being more like two and a half hours. We sat there sweating in the notary office as the temperature was consistently in the 90s every day. Once the paperwork was complete, he took us shopping at the department store once again. We bought Kaia another outfit and a new sippy cup. In three days she'd already chewed a hole in the previous cup. With her cleft palate, she wasn't able to suck well, so she chewed on the tip to get the liquids out. Actually, Kyle came up with a much better alternative to the sippy cup issue. Kaia was used to her cleft palate bottle, which she squeezed with her hands to get the liquid out. Kyle took a pin and poked multiple holes in the cap of a water bottle and Kaia was able to squeeze the water bottle and easily get water to drink. His little invention worked great! I think people thought we were crazy giving our child a water bottle with the cap on; little did they know water was actually coming out. We used this technique for the remainder of our time in China for all of her beverages.

Knowing that tomorrow was our last day, Frank was trying to smooth things over. He offered to take us to a restaurant to eat that night. We went to the Three Pot restaurant for soup. It was a very crowded restaurant and everyone's attention seemed to turn to us once we walked in. Several men spoke to Frank, and Kyle asked him what they said. They were asking why the Americans have Chinese babies and Frank's reply to them was, "Not Chinese babies. American babies." I'm pretty sure they didn't buy that answer, but it was very evident that most of the Chinese people in this area had no idea about the children in the orphanage and international adoption. We were taken upstairs and walked through another crowded dining room. I held Kaia tight to my chest and walked as fast as I could to avoid the stares. We were taken to a small private room with one round table. Frank ordered for us. We had a variety of food including duck broth soup, eggplant potato stir-fry, beef and onion, fried rice, and mixed vegetables. Kaia couldn't get enough of the duck broth soup. Every once in awhile I'd find actual duck parts and would quietly set them to the side. It was the best meal we'd had while in Yinchuan and the least expensive; it came to $4 per person. It was getting late, so we headed back to the hotel. Tomorrow was a big day; we had to be at the police station at 9:30 A.M. to pick up Kaia's passport and then off to the airport for our 1:00 P.M. flight to Guangzhou. It appeared that the duck broth soup didn't agree with Kaia because before she even fell asleep that night she developed diarrhea. We'd now done a complete 180-degree turn from constipation to diarrhea. This wasn't just loose BMs; it was full-on watery diarrhea. All I could think was, *Great—now I really have to push the fluids to avoid dehydration.*

We got Kaia to sleep and finished packing for the next leg of our trip. We were so excited to be going to Guangzhou the next day. We'd felt so isolated and out of place here, having a computer with Internet access was one of the few things that helped keep our sanity and feel a little closer to home. Twenty minutes after Kaia fell asleep, the crying spells started again. She would cry out and flail around almost in a seizure-like activity but never was she fully awake. This would last for about five minutes; she'd settle down, and the cycle would repeat itself all over again. We had ignorantly thought this was due to constipation the night before, but I knew now that these were night terrors. She flailed about so much that we had to put pillows up against the wall to protect her from getting hurt.

I had some knowledge about these, and most of the literature said not to wake the child, just protect them from harming themselves. We tried about every tactic I could think of, but nothing worked. The night terrors were every twenty to thirty minutes without fail, and she was inconsolable. It was about 3:00 A.M. before I completely broke down. I couldn't help but ask myself, *Have I made a mistake?* This child was clearly emotionally scarred, thought it was funny to harm me, was displaying autistic-type behaviors, and was very mentally and physically delayed. I had two other children at home to think about too. *Will this child require round-the-clock care? Will she be a danger to herself and others?* I'd hit my breaking point. I remember pacing around the room crying and telling Kyle, "I'm sorry if I've screwed up our life and our family. Things are never going to be the same again." It was 3:00 A.M., and I was sleep deprived and emotionally stressed to the max; I wasn't thinking rationally. Kyle did his best to keep me grounded and reassured me things will be fine, but I know he had to be having those same thoughts at that point in time. I eventually settled down, and we got as much sleep as possible in twenty-minute intervals.

Night Terrors

Definition: Night terrors are described as frequent recurrent episodes of intense crying and fear during sleep. The child may thrash and scream. Often the child appears awake but does not speak or respond to stimuli or comforting from the parents. These children may also experience increased heart rate, breathing rate, and sweating. The episode usually lasts a few minutes, but can extend to thirty minutes before the child returns to normal sleep. Usually, the child has no recollection of the event.

Causes: Causes are unknown but seem to be triggered by stressful life events, fever, and sleep deprivation.

Treatment: There is no treatment. Parents are advised to keep a consistent bedtime routine and keep the child's room as safe as possible to avoid injury during a night terror. If night terrors persist, talk to your doctor as testing may be necessary to rule out other causes.

Prognosis: Children usually outgrow the terrors by adolescence or when a known stressor is removed.

∾ **Day 8** ∾

Despite another sleepless night, we woke with positive thoughts because we would be leaving for Guangzhou today. Our hotel room had started to feel more like a prison cell than a hotel room. I jumped in the shower while Kaia slept, but before I finished, she woke up. Kyle picked her up, and she allowed him to hold her, but as soon as I stepped out of the bathroom she couldn't get from Kyle to me fast enough. The fact that she let Kyle hold her even for a few minutes was a major event. We then proceeded to have breakfast and finished packing. We waited in the hotel lobby for our guide to pick us up. As we stood there waiting, Kaia stood next to me and swayed back and forth in a rhythmic motion. I'd noticed that she did this often, but didn't think much about it until Zoe started to mimic Kaia. This made Diane very uncomfortable. She told Zoe to stop, and they walked away from us. It may seem insignificant to many, but to me it was her way of saying, "That little girl is not normal. You don't want to play with her." I know that Kaia has a lifetime ahead of her as being "different"; she'll be the only Asian kid in her school, she's adopted, and she's going to have difficulties with speech, but I didn't expect her to be ostracized quite so soon.

Our guide was right on time, and we boarded the bus to the police station. We were told the orphanage director would meet us there. Once again it was just a short drive away. We were walking on the sidewalk outside the police station, holding the girls in our arms, when we noticed a woman hiding behind a vehicle. She was watching us and crying hysterically. Next to her was a man I assume her husband and one of the caretakers from the orphanage. I recognized the caretaker as the one who brought Kaia to us on adoption day. She was doing her best to comfort the woman, but the woman was crying like she'd just been told the most tragic news. It was then that we realized she was Zoe's foster mom. They had come here to see Zoe one last time. The foster mother did not allow Zoe to see her, as not to upset Zoe. It was obvious that this woman cared deeply for the child, and it was heart wrenching to see the sadness in her face. Zoe was very lucky to have been placed with a foster family that loved her so much. I looked at Kaia and felt sadness for her that she hasn't had anyone to love her with such intensity. To this day I still wonder if the caretaker was there to see Kaia or just to provide comfort to the foster mom. I'd like to think that Kaia and this caretaker had an attachment and bond, but I will never know.

We sat in the police station and waited for the passports. With its rows of chairs, the room reminded me of a secretary of state's office. As we sat there waiting, I turned around and looked toward the street. The foster mom was outside with her face pressed against the window, hands cupped around her eyes still trying to see Zoe. She was still crying, but not so vehemently. It was torture to watch this woman suffer. Our guide and the orphanage director spoke to a police officer and shortly after that she came over to us and handed us the girls' passports. We were now officially done in Yinchuan.

From there, we went directly to the airport, which was about a thirty-five minute drive. We went over the Yellow River, and I took in as much as I could from the drive because we never really got to see the area Kaia was from. There was a gift shop at the airport, so we bought a few things there. It was fortunate that most of the items were handmade items from that province, so I was happy to have the opportunity to buy some keepsakes for Kaia that were from her province in China. We bought some scarves and a leather skirt/dress for Kaia that was 100 percent handmade so no two were alike. We said our good-byes to our guide.

We gave Frank a thank-you note and also a good tip for his services. During our time in Yinchuan, we learned the location that Kaia was found. We hoped to visit the location, but Frank informed us the city was 200 kilometers away, and there would be no way that we could go there. He did inform us that he usually goes there in the spring and would take pictures of the location for us. Knowing he was our only hope at another glimpse of Kaia's past, we made sure he got a good tip and our contact information in case he chose to follow through on his promise. (The following year we received an e-mail from Frank with several pictures of Kaia's finding spot, and for that we will always be grateful.)

Our flight had a brief stop in Xian, but I couldn't have been happier with the flight from Yinchuan to Xian. Kaia was very good and even ate most of her airline lunch tray; the rest she threw on the floor. We got off the plane in Xian for about twenty minutes and then re-boarded the same plane. The second leg of our flight didn't go as well. Kaia had her own seat but refused to sit in it. She preferred to stand, which was not an option. I had to hold her on my lap because she refused to sit still, and she screamed for about ten to fifteen minutes before she finally fell asleep. She was exhausted as it was about 2:00 P.M., and she usually napped in the late morning. The whole plane breathed a sigh of relief when she finally fell asleep. The only problem with her sleeping was that she started having night terrors. The flight lasted about two and a half hours, and she had five night terrors during that time. Each one lasted about five minutes and she would scream, cry, and flail but never really wake up. All the while we sat there feeling helpless and empathetic to our fellow passengers.

Kaia woke up shortly before the plane landed, and she once again had a fever. We landed in Guangzhou and our new guide, Helen, was right there to meet us. We grabbed our luggage and headed toward the Holiday Inn Shifu, our "home" for the next five days. In the first fifteen minutes that we were with Helen, we knew we were blessed with a wonderful guide. She was very informative, compassionate, and knowledgeable. My anxieties about this new city melted away. She checked us into our room and gave us an itinerary for the next five days. She even took Kyle for a short walk to buy us some food as we were starving by then. I stayed back at the hotel with Kaia as she wasn't feeling well. A short while later, Kyle and Helen came back with Pizza Hut pizza and McDonald's French fries! I was never so excited to see comfort food from home! The three of us sat on the floor and devoured an entire large pizza, and Kaia enjoyed her first taste of McDonald's fries. I knew things would be better from now on.

By later that night, Kaia was feeling better again. She was quite active, and we played peek-a-boo behind the bed, which produced some much-needed smiles. She was really starting to warm up to Kyle. She even let him hold her for her nighttime bottle. Daddy held her twice today! This was by far our best day yet with our new daughter. It was hard to believe how much difference one day could make. Our hotel room was large. It had a king bed, couch, chair, desk, and lots of room to crawl around and play. It also had a full bathroom with bathtub, instead of just a shower stall like the last hotel. We had a crib brought in thinking that Kaia might sleep in that, but when we tried to put her in it, she became frantic. She screamed with terror, and it was clear that she would *not* be sleeping in the crib. We suspect it reminded her of her crib in the orphanage, but again like the night terrors, we don't know what thoughts were going through her mind. She proceeded to sleep between us in our king size bed for the rest of our time in China.

༄ Day 9 ༄

We woke with excitement knowing that we'd be reunited with our entire travel group today. Tim, Kristen, and their son Jamison arrived late the night before. We were anxious to meet Jamison and see how things were going for them. Unfortunately, when Kaia woke she had another fever of 102. I forced the Ibuprofen down her as today was the medical exam, and I didn't want her to fail because of a fever. After getting dressed, we went down for buffet breakfast. It was wonderful! There was definitely an American feel here. They had eggs, bacon, and French toast, as well as the traditional Chinese favorites. There were many Americans in the restaurant with their adoptive children as well. Most Americans that adopt in China have to come to Guangzhou as this is where the U.S. Embassy is located and where the adoption is finalized. Thus many adoptive families were staying at this hotel. We no longer felt so out of place.

After breakfast we met up with the rest of the group in Diane and Zoe's room. Helen met us there and helped us fill out the embassy-required paperwork and pay the final fees. From there, we boarded the bus and went to Sha Mian Island for visa photos and medical exams. The visa photos were uneventful, but the medical exam was downright traumatic. All children that are adopted from China have to go through this required medical exam. The facility was not large, but full of adoptive families and their children. It was loud and chaotic. There were three stations: vital signs, ENT (ear, nose and throat), and a brief exam by a medical doctor. We waited in line at each station as they moved us through like a herd of cattle. It was a very professional environment. All the staff members wore white lab coats and everything was stainless steel. The walls were bare white.

For Kaia, this was the scariest place in the world. It obviously reminded her of previous encounters with the medical community. Anytime someone tried to touch her or examine her, she screamed and trembled in such terror. There were times that she cried so hard that she nearly quit breathing or I thought she would vomit. Even getting her height was a challenge. She did reach for me, which was comforting to know that she had started to form a bond with me. The exams were very cursory at best. I can't imagine that many children fail. Kaia passed, but by the time we left her clothes were saturated in sweat, and she was exhausted from the screaming and crying. I was exhausted, too. It was very difficult to see her so fearful. *What has this little girl gone through?* I thought.

We had the option to stay on the island and shop, but Kaia was still upset and tired from the ordeal, so we opted to go back to the hotel. We all had a much-needed nap. After Kaia woke, she was much happier, and even let Kyle hold her again. We met up with the Healey family and ventured out of our hotel to check out the shops. Our hotel was located in a shopping district. It was on a pedestrian-only part of the street. The streets were lined with stores and the side streets were also lined with small specialty shops. Some streets seemed to have a specialty. There was one street that had mostly pets for sale. These were not tourist shops by any means; in fact, there were very few tourists here. This was where the locals shopped, and there was always an abundance of people in the streets.

The shops on Sha Mian Island were more touristy as they catered to adoptive families. Many adoptive families stay at hotels on the island, but the major one was under construction when we were there. In hindsight, I'm glad we stayed off the island as our hotel room was wonderful, and we also got a taste for some traditional culture. We found a large department store and bought some outfits for Kaia. We managed quite well on our own, but I noticed that many of the shopkeepers did make attempts at speaking English (or Chinglish as our guide put it) as they were more accustomed to seeing Americans here. The shopkeepers would often follow us around trying to convince us to buy something. They were happy to barter and carried around a calculator to show us how many yuan something cost. Kaia did well. She wasn't fazed in the least by all the people. The massive crowds of people everywhere were what amazed me the most. Our guide told us that Guangzhou was a small city of only nine million people. Nine million! I come from a town that has less people than the hotel where I was staying, so the population was mind-boggling. Unfortunately, the poverty was also evident as it is in any large city.

Gift Ideas When in Country

Many adoptive families celebrate the adoption day (or "gotcha day" as some prefer) every year just as you would a birthday. Some families have been creative and bought enough gifts or trinkets from China to present one item to their child every year on their adoption day. It's an excellent way keep the child's culture alive and spark discussions of the adoption day. Major life events such as a graduation or wedding would also make excellent opportunities to present gifts from the homeland.

That night Helen took our group to dinner at the Guangzhou Restaurant. As Kyle described it, it was 150 yards and 250 stores away from our hotel. It is a very well-known restaurant specializing in traditional Cantonese food. The restaurant was very large and busy. There was a large birthday celebration for an elder and that kept the wait staff very busy. In China, elders are treated with utmost respect, and thus their party took priority over our table. Regardless of our long wait, the food was excellent. Kaia was in an especially good mood. She ate her usual bowl of congee, but then proceeded to feed herself green beans and rice. She was smiling and much of the rice got flung onto the floor, but we couldn't have been happier because she was happy and feeding herself.

When we finally left the restaurant, it was raining. Kaia giggled when the raindrops fell on her head. By now, Kyle and I were giddy with excitement because our little girl seemed truly happy. We got some pictures of her smiling. We had to be sneaky about it because every time we lifted the camera to take her picture she'd stop smiling and close her eyes. It was bedtime now, so we decided to try out the bathtub. I wasn't sure what to expect. She was scared of grass, cameras, the crib, and Kyle, so I was concerned the bath and water may upset her, too. I was wrong. She had a blast in the bathtub. I took a bath with her so she wouldn't be scared, but clearly that wasn't necessary. She played and splashed until the water turned cold. It was the perfect end to a great day. She had some warm milk and was off to sleep.

∽ Day 10 ∽

Another restless night. Kaia was no longer running a fever, but she was still coughing a lot at night and still having the night terrors. I can't count how many times Kyle and I were kicked or hit during a night terror when she flailed about. However, we had noticed that the night terrors were improving. She was only having them every hour or so instead of every twenty to thirty minutes.

Our day started off as per usual with a shower and hotel buffet breakfast. Helen took us on a sightseeing/shopping trip. Kaia was getting very heavy to carry around, so Helen brought us a borrowed stroller to use when we were out sightseeing. We put Kaia in it, and she freaked out again. She was screaming and carrying on. There were many people around, and my first instinct was to take her out, but Helen told me, "No. Leave her in there. She'll get used to it." I guess I was worried what the other Chinese people would think. I didn't want them thinking I was being mean to one of their children, but Helen, being a mom herself, was very reassuring. Kaia did settle down, and I held her hand while Kyle pushed her in the stroller. After that first time, she was fine with the stroller the rest of the week.

Our first stop was a Chinese folk art museum. The intricate carving and engravings on the buildings were amazing. There were some local artists there as well. We bought a painted scroll and the artist painted Kaia's Chinese and American names on it. It hangs in her room to this day. From there we went to a shopping plaza that I think was reserved for adoptive parents. There was a little bit of everything here: porcelain, jade, silk clothes, souvenirs, etc. It did seem a bit pricier, but the quality was good, and it was all in one location. We bought a small porcelain tea set and three silk outfits for Kaia to wear as she gets older. Kyle also bought her a small jade bangle. It was explained to us that jade is considered good luck. Because of feng shui, positive energy enters the left arm and negative energy leaves out the right; thus, jade is always worn on the left arm. After spending way too much money, we headed back to the hotel. It was still in the upper 90s every day, and the rooftop pool was sounding good. We donned our swimsuits and met the Healeys at the pool. Jamison, being a bit older, was having a blast. Kaia did not have any issues with the pool, but she was getting very tired, so our swim was short but sweet.

We had no further appointments that day, so we relaxed in the hotel room. Kyle was thrilled because there were some American movies and TV shows to watch here in Guangzhou. Kaia did well the rest of the day. She was playing and interacting much more. Her fever seemed to be gone for good, and you could tell she was feeling better. She was eating like crazy. In fact she and Jamison both seemed to have some eating issues. At dinner one night, Jamison ate so much that he got sick and vomited. Kaia was nearly doing the same. They were both from orphanages and didn't know how to stop eating. We had to limit the amount of food they ate to avoid overeating. Sometimes we'd bring a banana back to the room, and I'd give it to Kaia for a mid-afternoon snack. Each time she had a banana, she'd hold the last bite in her mouth for what seemed like an eternity. She held it in her mouth for forty-five minutes once. I guess she was savoring that last bite because she wasn't sure when the next meal would be. She did seem overwhelmed by the variety of foods offered but never passed anything up. We did receive a handwritten sheet of paper from the orphanage that Helen interpreted for us. It included information on her diet and language. It read as follows:

Meals: Three times per day. A small bowl of rice for each meal. To have the water and snacks for several times.

Further, two times for formula for the early morning and the late night. About 250ml (approximately an eight-ounce bottle) of formula/time.

Language: 'Til now, she can only call "mama" and "ayi" {aunty}, however she is eager to get the other's attention.

Things were getting much better in China, but I was missing my boys back home. I talked to them almost daily, but the separation was more difficult each day. They asked a lot of questions about Kaia and truly seemed excited to meet her. When we talked to them we put the phone up to her ear so she could hear them, but the boys were disappointed that she wasn't talking to them. They didn't quite understand why Kaia was unable to speak to them. The countdown had begun—three more days until we were home.

∾ Day 11 ∾

This was basically a free day. Helen had to present our paperwork to the Embassy for Kaia's final visa approval at 11:00 A.M. We did not have to appear in person, but we were to wait in our rooms just in case they had any questions. Shortly after 11:00, Helen called to inform us everything went well, and we were free to enjoy the rest of the day because tomorrow Kaia would be sworn in as a U.S. citizen.

Once we got the green light, we jumped in a cab and headed for Sha Mian Island to do some sightseeing and shopping. We started out at the famous White Swan Hotel.

It was very nice inside. In the lobby of the White Swan are red couches where adoptive families often take pictures of the children; they are famously referred to as "red couch pictures." I thought, *What the heck. Let's get a red couch picture too.* We plopped Kaia and Zoe on a red couch and snapped a few pictures. There were many shops on the ground floor of the hotel that had some really nice things. I bought a beautifully decorated kite to hang in Kaia's room.

Figure 8: Kaia on the famous red couch at the White Swan Hotel.

Once we stepped out onto the street, we encountered shop after shop full of souvenirs and items for our little girls. It was evident that these shops were destined for adoptive families because I didn't see *any* local Chinese people shopping there; they were all over by our hotel off the island. I must admit, we did have fun shopping that day. We bought Kaia some squeaky shoes that later drove us crazy, but it seemed like the thing to do at the time. We bought souvenirs for the boys and for us. We bought another carry-on piece of luggage for Kaia that cost less than $20. Since she had her own seat on the plane, we were able to bring another piece of luggage home. It was a good thing because we needed it for all the souvenirs we bought. At one of the last stores, we ran into Tim and Kristen. It started to rain, so we waited for a cab to take us back to the hotel. We all crammed into the same cab together. Thankfully we didn't have far to go because we had four adults, two children, one umbrella stroller, two backpacks, and two pieces of carry-on luggage that we had to cram into one cab no larger than an Escort. The cab fare was a whopping $1.

When we got back we were all starving and craving some familiar food. McDonald's was just a five-minute walk from the hotel, and it was calling our names. The menu was very similar to ours at home. We couldn't read the menu, but we just pointed at the Value Meal we wanted. We did have to be careful to order the "American style" Big Mac that was made with Thousand Island dressing. Their Big

Mac was made with soy sauce. Fast food has never tasted so good! Some of us even went back for seconds. We all left there very satisfied. On the walk back to the hotel, we took our time and stopped at a few of the shops, but we were ready for a quiet night and some relaxation. We put our purchases away, and I asked Kaia if she wanted to take a bath. Much to our surprise, she walked right into the bathroom as if to say, *Heck yeah, I want a bath!* I was very excited at the prospect that she'd learned that word already; maybe the speech and language barrier wouldn't be so bad after all.

After bath time she turned into the "terrible-two toddler" again. I caught her putting a toy in the toilet, and when I told her no and scolded her, she just laughed and did it again. When I tried to stop her from doing something naughty, she'd slap me. Don't get me wrong, things were improving every day, but she was still displaying many *orphanage behaviors* as we called them. We put Kaia to bed, but each night the task became more difficult.

Orphanage Behaviors

This is a term that I use to bundle some of the characteristics we observed in Kaia. As most research will describe, institutionalized children are often emotionally immature and will go to great lengths to get attention from a caretaker. The following list includes some common behaviors found in those children who have lived in orphanages. Obviously, every situation is different and thus not every child that has lived in an orphanage will have issues, but we experienced firsthand many of these behaviors.

- Hoarding of food and toys

- Stealing and lying

- Rocking and/or head banging

- Loud and attention-getting behavior

- Night terrors

- Abusiveness

- Tantrums

- Attachment disorders

Thankfully, most of these disappear as the child adjusts to their new family but prove to be a challenge for parents nonetheless.

∞ Day 12 ∞

Our last full day in China! We slept in later than normal today, and when we went down to breakfast, the familiar hostess and wait staff greeted us. By now we were "regulars," and they didn't even need to ask us our room number or name anymore. They all knew who we were. We had all morning to ourselves. The swearing in ceremony at the U.S. Embassy wasn't until 2:30 P.M. We walked for two hours up and down the side streets. The streets were lined with small family-owned stores and vendors. The streets were dirty and the farther we walked from the hotel, poverty became more and more evident. The smells weren't very pleasing either. It was hot and crowded, and we discovered deodorant isn't as widely used in China as it is here in the States. The smells became worse the closer we were to our hotel. Right next to our hotel entrance was a street vendor cooking beef, pork, and squid. The smell was pungent—a cross between sewage and spicy meat being seared on a greasy grill.

Kaia was able to take a short nap before we headed off to the U.S. Embassy for our swearing in ceremony. As I recall, it was about a thirty-minute bus ride from the hotel. We went through a security station and into a large room with approximately forty other adoptive families. Again, it was a bit chaotic with that many young children, but it was kid-friendly with toys and small chairs for the children to sit and play. At the time of the swearing in, we all had to stand, raise our right hands, and recite after the official. We had to swear to raise the children in a loving home and never to harm or abandon them. I'm pretty sure there was more to it, but I can't remember everything that was said. What I do remember is being moved to tears when it was complete, and they said, "Congratulations, you are now officially new parents, and as soon as you touch American soil, they will become American citizens." It had finally happened. After so much time, she was finally ours. It was official! We received a brown envelope that we were told to guard with our life. We were given explicit instructions not to open it, and we were to give this sealed envelope to the customs and immigration agent once we arrived in the United States. This was it—the culmination of over a year's worth of waiting.

Our bus ride back to the hotel took much longer due to rush hour traffic. Helen told us it was a city of nine million people and one million cars. Motorcycles were banned earlier in the year because motorcycle accidents accounted for nearly 75 percent of hospital admissions. Two women were also dragged to death as a result of motorcycle purse-snatching incidents. According to Helen, traffic was much better now. It was hard to believe it was any better because riding in the bus was still downright scary. At any given time, you could reach your hand out the bus window and touch the vehicle next to you.

When we arrived back at the hotel, we took a family picture with Helen to remember her since she had been so helpful. I've heard many horror stories about adoptions that don't go as planned because of paperwork or other unforeseen problems. I have to say our adoption went exactly as planned. The paperwork was in order and all of our appointments went as scheduled. We had no unexpected issues, and for that I was thankful.

To celebrate, we went out to dinner with the Healy's at Pizza Hut. It wasn't the most enjoyable meal. Both Kaia and Jamison started to act out. Kaia had an absolute meltdown. She threw anything she could get her hands on including food and silverware. We basically ate and left as soon as possible. We went back to the hotel to start packing since our bus would pick us up at 5:45 A.M. the next morning to take us to the airport. I was happy to get back to the hotel room because I also started feeling poorly. Most people worry about getting traveler's diarrhea, right? No, not me. I was miserably constipated. I'd only been constipated like that two other times in my life—both times after I had delivered the boys. I assumed it was due to having a vaginal delivery, but here I was feeling the same way after the gift of my third child. Don't get me wrong, it wasn't nearly as physically painful, but emotionally I was going through hell. I was in a foreign country away from family and friends, and we had a toddler instead of a newborn. Newborns basically eat, sleep, poop, and cry. You nurture them and repeat the cycle over and over. The gift of my third child was different since she was a toddler— old enough to be angry, fearful, and apprehensive, but too young to understand that we would be her forever family and would love and care for her unconditionally. She was already set in her ways, had her routines, her familiar foods, her language, and her culture. Life as she knew it changed the day we arrived, and she felt the need to punish us.

∾ Day 13 ∾

We woke at 4:45 A.M. to shower and head for home. I barely slept at all that night because I was so excited to be going home. I looked at the alarm clock every hour scared to oversleep and miss our flight. Our entire group was leaving at the same time. Tim and Kristen were on a different flight than the rest of us. We left the hotel later than planned because Diane was running behind. The hotel packed us a light breakfast to eat on the ride to the airport. We were so excited to be heading for home. Once we got to the airport, Helen helped each of us check in, and we said our good-byes. We had arrived there late, and there were long lines. Thankfully, we were allowed to cut to the front of the lines in security because we had small children. It was a good thing because when we got to our gate, our plane was already half full. As our plane taxied out onto the runway, I was so excited to be going home, but I also felt a deep sadness for Kaia. She was too young to comprehend what was happening, but I was sad for her. She was leaving her country, the country where she was born, a country where she looked like everyone else. This was her homeland, and I was taking her from here. Leaving was bittersweet.

This was a three hour and forty-five minute flight to Tokyo, and then on to Detroit. Kaia did fairly well on that flight. She had a snack, some milk, and even took a short nap. Once we got to Tokyo, we thought we had a layover of an hour and a half, but we completely forgot about there being a time change. We really only had forty-five minutes. Kaia and I sat at the gate while Kyle went to the bathroom. Apparently, he was wandering around looking for snacks thinking he had lots of time. They started boarding the plane and still no Kyle. *Where was he?* The thought of missing our plane was incomprehensible. We were this close to going home, and the thought of a long layover was more than I could handle. My mind began racing, and I was starting to freak out, when finally he came, and we proceeded onto the plane with the last few passengers. Whew!

The next flight was miserable. I was still not feeling well, and Kaia decided again that she wanted nothing to do with Kyle. She had her own seat on the plane, but refused to sit in it. She was tired as were Kyle and I. She eventually fell asleep on my lap, but if I even moved in the slightest, she went into a night terror. We lost track of how many times that happened on that flight. I never slept more than thirty minutes without interruption. At the front of the plane was a TV screen showing our current location. I got to the point where I forced myself not to look at it anymore because I was convinced we weren't getting anywhere. I was starting to go out of my mind. I would have given anything to stretch my legs and sleep.

I loathed the people in first class, and I'm sure everyone around me loathed us, too.

The flight was pure torture—a true test of determination. The only positive thing that happened on that flight was Kaia drank two and a half bottles of milk, for which we were thankful. That was the most she'd had in a day since we got her. Seventeen hours after leaving our hotel, we were now descending into Detroit, Michigan. It was about 1:00 P.M., but because of the twelve-hour time difference, it was still the same day. I was never so happy to be in Detroit. Once we deplaned, we had to go straight to immigration. We handed over Kaia's brown envelope and after being ushered through a couple of different lines, we finally received the all-important stamp on her passport. Without cracking a smile, the immigration agent looked at Kaia, and in the most dry, monotone voice said, "Welcome to the U.S. kid." Tears of joy ran down my face. I looked at Kaia and said, "Welcome home, Kaia!" Everything was final. She was officially our child, and she was a U.S. citizen.

We couldn't pass through customs fast enough because I knew my sister and her husband were there to pick us up and had brought Mason and Max with them. I requested that she bring the boys to the airport because I couldn't wait another minute to see them. We came around the corner, and there they were. My boys looked so good. Max looked like he had aged six months. Max walked right up to Kaia, gave her a hug and said, "Hi, Kaia!" I didn't want to stop hugging them because I missed them so much. We called my mom to tell her that we were home safe, and she started crying. I fully expected that response as my mother was very nervous about us traveling so far from home, but I was awfully happy to hear her voice as well. We loaded our things in the car. I expected Kaia to throw a fit when I put her in the car seat, but much to my surprise, she didn't fight it at all. Not bad for her first encounter with a car seat. It's about a two-hour drive from the airport to our home. We were hungry and stopped at Subway to eat. Oh how I'd missed the food from home.

There were two surprises for us when we got home. With the help of our babysitter, the boys had decorated the house for our homecoming, and my girlfriends had decorated Kaia's bedroom while we were gone. We received the clearance to travel so much faster than expected that I didn't get the opportunity to paint and decorate Kaia's room before we left. While we were gone, my wonderful friends came in and painted her room, decorated the walls and bought clothes, books, etc. What a relief that I didn't have to do it, and they did a much better job that I ever could have. I'm truly blessed with great friends and family.

Later that day, our immediate family came over to welcome us home. Kaia still didn't want anything to do with Kyle or any other man for that matter, but she was fine around her brothers. She actually seemed relaxed. It made sense when we thought about it. She was used to living in a crowded orphanage with lots of other children, but for the past two weeks she was stuck primarily with adults. Having her brothers made the transition so much easier. She trusted them because they were kids like her, and she watched them hug and kiss and play with Kyle and me. You could almost see her thinking, *Hmm, these guys seem to love and trust them, and maybe I should, too.*

She was also fascinated by some of our toys. The first toy she played with was Mr. Potato Head. She didn't know what she was supposed to do with the pieces, but she was very intrigued by it. Mostly, she just watched Mason and Max play.

We had a beloved family pet. He was a large golden retriever named Buddy. We always joked that Buddy was our firstborn child. He was a great dog—childproof you might say. Buddy stayed with my in-laws while we were gone, and they brought him back home that night. With the exception of Kaia, we were all so happy to see him. Buddy was an eighty-pound puffball of excitement to see us, too. After he and Kyle wrestled around for a bit, he calmed down and walked over to Kaia to get a sniff. Kaia just about jumped out of her skin. When he got close, she screamed and trembled with fear, begging me to pick her up. We tried to convince her that Buddy was a nice dog, but she wasn't buying it. She was completely fearful of Buddy if he was even in the same room as her. To her, he was a scary monster. We also have a small outside cat, named Dora. Dora came to the back sliding door, and Kaia went into hysterics all over again. It only took two days for Kaia to warm up to Buddy and Dora, but for those first two days, we tried to keep Buddy in a room opposite of Kaia.

By evening, we were exhausted. It had been about thirty hours since we last slept, and I was in desperate need of sleep. It would have been very easy to just place her in bed with us that night, but that was one habit that I didn't want to start. I had borrowed a toddler bed from one of my friends for Kaia to sleep in. She had a room to herself, but I didn't want her to feel alone, so we blew up an air mattress and laid it right next to her bed. I put Kaia in her bed, and I slept on the mattress. I was right next to her and laid my hand on her back until she fell asleep. I slept there all night so that I'd be there for the night terrors and when she woke. There were night terrors that night. She woke at about 2:30 A.M. ready to play. Remember, we are now twelve hours different from what she was used to. However, the lack of sleep didn't seem to matter as much because we were finally home.

CHAPTER 6

The First Month Home

Kaia progressed quite nicely over the next few weeks. I took two weeks off work to stay at home to help her adjust and to facilitate attachment and bonding. Kyle's employer offered a total of five weeks off for adoption leave, so when I went back to work, he was able to stay home another few weeks. Initially I was concerned that she wasn't attaching well enough. Sure, she'd want me if she was scared or hungry, but she was just as happy to go to another female even if she didn't know her. I'd read about this before we traveled, so we tried to limit the amount of people who held her those first few weeks home. The most difficult part was that she still wasn't going to Kyle. She may not have been able to talk, but she was very clear in letting us know that she did not want Kyle to hold her or do anything for her. I know it was very difficult for Kyle; it was difficult for me to watch. I'm sure he was thinking, *Look kid, I've traveled around the world for you and made more sacrifices than you know—you better start liking me!*

Figure 9: Photograph of Kaia and her brothers taken during the first week home.

Adjusting at Home

Most newly adoptive parents think that once they return home with their new child things will get easier, when in reality it can get more difficult for the child. They may have just started to accept you, and now they are thrown into a completely different environment. If adopting internationally, the food will be different, all of the people will look and sound different, and there will be a different bed to sleep in and possibly in a much different time zone. I believe the first few weeks home can be the most challenging for both child and parent. Here are a few tips to help with the transition:

- Limit visitors the first few weeks home and only allow immediate family members to hold the child.

- Meet the child's needs as soon as possible.

- Don't stop bottle feeding right away.

- Avoid overstimulation. Avoid large family gatherings, trips to amusement parks, etc.

- Do not allow the child to cry himself or herself to sleep—he or she needs to feel comforted.

- Develop a daily routine. Children adjust faster if they know what to expect.

- Develop rules and stick with them. If the child misbehaves, avoid time-outs where the child is placed out of your sight. Instead, give them a time-in, where they are placed near you. Never allow the child to feel alone.

My sleeping technique was working well. I slept right next to her for the first few nights, and then I moved the air mattress away from her bed, so that we couldn't touch. She could still see me, but I was slowly working my way out of her room. I did this for another week. Once she fell asleep, I went to my own bed. I left her door open and could easily hear her when she woke up. After about two weeks, I took the air mattress out of her room. I put her to bed and sat right outside her room in the hall. She could still see me, but I did not enter the room. After another two and a half weeks, I was able to put her to bed and walk away without any issues. It also helped that she was on the same routine as her brothers. She saw them brush their teeth and go to bed, so she followed suit. After about three weeks, the night terrors were nearly gone. She would still have an occasional one, but there were more nights without than with the night terrors.

Kaia turned into an eating machine. There wasn't a food that she would turn down. I had no troubles getting her to eat a balanced diet. We could only give her soft foods because of the large cleft palatal defect, but she could eat meat, pizza, vegetables, and fruit without a problem. In the first two weeks we were home, she gained two pounds. She was still just a mere twenty-two pounds, but we were moving in the right direction. It didn't take us long to realize eating was becoming an obsession for Kaia. She wanted to eat all day long. As soon as she woke in the morning, she pointed at the cabinet where the oatmeal was. She always wanted more food even if she still had food on her plate. She could be full but if someone was eating in the same room, she thought she should be eating, too. She had obviously gone hungry before and hadn't yet realized that she would now always have enough food to eat.

Post-Adoption Medical Care

After returning home with your child, make an appointment with a pediatrician right away because a complete history and physical examination, including blood work, hearing and vision screening, and developmental assessments are recommended. It is recommended to repeat all pre-adoption blood work, including screenings for diseases and lead levels. Some physicians also suggest repeating all immunizations that were given in a foreign country. Talk with your doctor about what is right for your child.

From a medical standpoint, she was also doing much better. Her cough was nearly gone. We'd been to the pediatrician several times. Other than signs of malnutrition, she was doing quite well. There was a concern that she may have rickets, but thankfully X-rays failed to document that. Her initial blood work was abnormal but improved within the next two weeks. Each time we went to a medical appointment, it was a major traumatic event all over again. She did not trust men; thankfully, our pediatrician is a woman. The first time she had blood work, they had trouble drawing it. Forty minutes later, I had a very sweaty and exhausted little girl. She cried the whole time.

We had our appointment at the cleft palate clinic. This is a multidisciplinary clinic that specializes in the care of a cleft-palate child. Our visit was scheduled for the entire morning, and during that appointment we saw a pediatrician, otolaryngology (ears, nose, and throat) physician, oral surgeon, plastic surgeon, dentist, dietician, social worker, and speech therapists. The surgeon told us he thought that the palate could be repaired in one surgery, but there was a 30 percent failure rate. She would need more oral surgery and bone grafting later on, but right now getting the palate closed was the priority. He opted to wait another one to two months before surgery to give her a chance to improve nutrition and adjust to her new surroundings. He informed us that after surgery, she would be in arm immobilizers (called "no-nos") for six weeks to prevent her from putting anything in her mouth. All it would take was one object in her mouth, and the repair could fail. She also would have to be drinking out of a cup because even a bottle would jeopardize the repair.

Normally, I would never want to see a two-year-old still drinking out of a bottle, but this was the only way Kaia knew how to drink. We'd tried different sippy cups and even just regular cups, but the liquid ended up pouring all over her. I had a month to get her drinking out of a cup before surgery. The nutrition/feeding specialists were amazed with the types of foods Kaia was able to eat. She'd adapted quite well. She was, however, still not muttering any sounds. The speech therapist recommended that we enroll Kaia in our county's Early Intervention program. After some pushing we finally got Kaia evaluated and with her delays both developmentally and with speech and language, she qualified for free in-home therapy.

Special Needs Services

If you suspect that your child has developmental delays, help is available through the Early Intervention program in your county. This is a federal program developed under the Individuals with Disabilities Act. Children from birth to age three are eligible for an evaluation and if necessary, treatment in the areas of speech, occupational, and physical therapy. Best of all, the program is usually free of cost, or at a very nominal fee. Talk to your pediatrician about making the referral; however, in some states, parents themselves can make the referral.

Kaia was dealing with a major life transition, but so were her two older brothers. Mason and Max coped very well with the adjustment. Not only did they have a new sister, but a sister with some special needs that were time consuming to a big brother fighting for mom and dad's affection. Kyle was able to spend a lot of time with the boys since Kaia still only wanted me. I'd be lying if I said it was easy. It wasn't. What I haven't mentioned is that my father died three months before traveling to China. My father and I were very close. I was still greiving when we went to adopt our little girl—the granddaughter he would never meet.

Life was not easy at this time. I was missing my father, and Mason was also having troubles dealing with the loss of his grandfather and having some troubles in school. I was still trying to get to know my new daughter and deal with tantrums, night terrors, and other orphanage behaviors. We were all trying to adjust to our new family, and even before we could get a handle on those things, Kaia was getting ready for a major surgery. I was back to work full-time, and things were taking their toll on my mental well-being. I was exhausted physically and emotionally.

I remember one Saturday when I sat on the floor in my room crying. Nothing major had happened that day; I just couldn't stop crying and couldn't bear to spend the day alone with my kids. I wasn't going to harm them; I never had those thoughts. I just didn't have the strength that day. Kyle was working, so I called my mom. I couldn't even speak, and all I did was cry. She graciously took the kids for the day. I cried on and off most of the day, but only had myself to take care of that day. Recognizing the symptoms, I worried that maybe I was slipping into a depression. With feelings of embarrassment, I went to the store and purchased an herbal antidepressant. I wasn't at the point that I needed to consult my physician, but thought maybe I could use a little extra help. It was a huge

step for me to acknowledge that maybe I
I'm a very independent person and ask fo
it worked out, I only took the pills for
then forgot about them. That day to my
therapeutic than any drug out there; it was a chance t
breakdown and "recharge." After a few days I was out of
my slump.

I was very fortunate that I did not slip into a depression,
but not everyone is as lucky as I am. I'm happy to see that
post-adoption depression is becoming a hot topic in the
adoption world. Most adoptive parents are embarrassed
to admit they are feeling sad or depressed because they've
been hoping and praying to become a parent for years.
I think they are afraid of people saying, "Why are you sad?
You finally got what you wanted." In fact this *is* what we
want, but some things don't come without taking a toll.
Most of the adoption literature is focused on what the
adoptive child is going through, but few take into account
the sacrifices and challenges that the parents endure. Post-
adoption depression is not something to be ashamed of.
It is a very real phenomenon, and newly adoptive parents
should feel no shame in asking for help. I remember sitting
on our front porch crying for no reason a few days after
having my second son. I didn't know why I was crying. It
was short-lived. I didn't have post-partum depression or
the baby blues for that matter. Did I have post-adoption
blues? Maybe.

Post-Adoption Depression

It's not often spoken about in the adoption world. As new parents we're supposed to be the happiest people on the planet. We've waited so long for this day to happen, but for some it's not the picture-perfect scenario. Contrary to what many believe, it's usually not love at first sight. Bonding and attachment take time. The child and parent alike are both going through a significant life transition that can take a great toll emotionally.

Tips to Combat Depression

- Accept help from others. Allow close friends and family members to help with chores around the house.

- Get plenty of sleep and exercise. Don't try to do too much.

- Take the child outside for walks. Fresh air can be very therapeutic.

- Join an adoptive support group.

- Talk openly about your feelings with your significant other; chances are he or she may be feeling the same way but is afraid to admit it.

Signs and Symptoms of Depression

- Depressed mood most days: feeling sad, empty, and tearful.

- Loss of interest in people and activities.

- Significant weight gain or loss.

- Difficulty sleeping or excessive sleep.

- Fatigue and loss of energy.

- Feelings of worthlessness, hopelessness, or guilt nearly every day.

- Thoughts about harming yourself or your child (seek help immediately).

If you are experiencing some of the above symptoms, consider consulting with your physician or mental health provider.

CHAPTER 7

Surgery

Approximately three months had passed since we arrived home, and we were getting ready to proceed with Kaia's surgery. In this time, we'd seen some major improvements. Kaia was now in love with her daddy. Her anxieties melted away, and she was just as happy with Kyle as with me. It was a huge relief for all of us. Her strength was also improving. Here was a child who couldn't crawl and could barely walk three months ago and was now running up and down the hall after her brothers. She was crawling and even able to crawl up on the couch by herself. I credit Mason and Max for her quick turnaround developmentally. If it weren't for them, I think she would have lagged behind much longer. She still wasn't speaking, but she was doing a lot of pointing and charades to get her point across. I'll never forget the day that she tattled on Mason without speaking a word.

All three kids were in the back room playing, and Kaia started crying. She came running in and motioned that she was hit in the head. When I asked her what happened, she grabbed my hand and took me in where Mason was playing and pointed at Mason and reenacted the hit to the head. When I asked Mason if he hit her, sure enough he had. While I wasn't pleased that Mason hit her on the head with a toy, I was overjoyed that Kaia was finally starting to communicate even if it was nonverbally.

She had a blast at Halloween. She was the cutest little ladybug you ever saw. She wore her squeaky shoes trick-or-treating, and we always knew where she was, but the squeaking did get a bit annoying by the end of the night. It only took a stop at one house, and Kaia had the idea of this trick-or-treating thing. By the end of the night, Mason was getting tired, but Kaia was still squeaking along going up and knocking on every door. She was finally at the point where she didn't fear the unknown every time something new came her way. She was finally starting to trust all of us; that was, until the surgery.

Surgery was scheduled for November 14. I had finally found a cup from which she could drink. It was a sippy cup made by Playtex, but it looked more like a travel cup. There was a small hole around the rim where the liquid came out. We removed the valve because she wasn't able to suck, and it worked great. In addition to the cleft palate repair that would be done by the plastic surgeon, she also needed tubes in her ears as she had failed all of the hearing tests. We were told that it is very common for cleft palate children to need tubes in their ears. Things were about to become very different for Kaia. She'd be able to hear better and hopefully be able to start speaking. And eating would be much easier. Kaia's cleft palate defect was quite large in my eyes (although I'm told they can be much larger). The opening in the roof of her mouth meant anytime her tongue would touch the top of her mouth, it would push the food and liquid out her nose. If she sneezed while eating, watch out! She'd adapted quite well. For instance, when she drank, she kept her mouth open, tilted her head back and sort of gulped the liquid. If you've ever tried to eat or drink without touching your tongue to the top of your mouth, you'll see it's not easy. She wasn't able to make many sounds because when she tried to speak, the air went out her nose. She was starting to say mama, but that was an easy sound because it does not require the tongue to come in contact with the palate. After surgery she would need to learn how to eat and drink all over again, and learn to speak for the first time.

Kyle and I took her to the hospital the morning of surgery. Kaia had no idea what to expect. I was thankful they chose not to start her IV until she was in the operating room. She went into surgery on time, and the ENT put the tubes in her ears first. He came out and told us everything went well, and the plastic surgeon had started working on the palate. We were to expect surgery to last about two hours. As with any mom, I was feeling sick to my stomach the entire time. Surgery is not a foreign place for me since I am a surgical PA, but it's always different when it's your child. I worried about her having an allergic reaction. They asked about her medical history, but we knew nothing. We knew she'd had surgery before in China to repair the cleft lip, but we didn't know if there were any complications or how she had handled it. We received no detailed information.

Shortly after two hours, her surgeon came out to speak with us. He was a man of few words, but said everything went well and that she'd be in pediatric ICU for the next two days. After about an hour, a nurse came for me to sit with Kaia in recovery. She took me to Kaia, and a nurse was holding her in a rocking chair. Kaia was crying. She had blood coming from her nose and her arm restraints were on. She looked terrible. I held her and tried to comfort her, but she was still groggy from the anesthesia. She'd fall asleep and then wake up crying. The crying turned into a very long night terror, and the nurses were concerned she was in severe pain, but I recognized this as a typical night terror for Kaia. I felt so bad for her. After about an hour, we were taken to our room in the pediatric ICU. She was to be monitored closely for postoperative bleeding and airway management. She did better than expected that day.

Later on the nurse told me I could try to give her something to drink. I was doubtful that she would, but I got her special cup out, and she drank without a problem. Right after that, she patted at her diaper. I took her to the bathroom, and she peed on the potty! Her diaper was hardly wet at all. I've failed to mention Kaia was nearly potty trained already. I think she was somewhat trained in the orphanage, but we usually kept her in pull-up diapers. She had very few accidents, and again her brothers played an important role. Every time she saw them go to the bathroom, she wanted to go as well. The only problem was we had to convince her that girls sit down to go potty! Regardless, I was so happy to see her drinking and going potty on her own.

The nurse told us that if she did well throughout the evening, we could take her down to the playroom. That is just what we did. The unit had plastic wagons that we could put her in and take her for a walk to the play area, and the nurses could monitor her remotely. She seemed happy to get out of her room, but she wasn't up to playing with toys. She just wanted to be held and had that lethargic look to her. We went back to the room because she was getting tired. We met a few other parents that night. Some of their children had been in the hospital for weeks with major medical problems. Although Kaia's issues were very real, they suddenly seemed minor when compared to these other children.

It was getting late, so I sent Kyle home to be with the boys and I spent the night with Kaia. She had to sleep in their hospital crib, which looks like a stainless steel cage, but she was tired and didn't fight it too hard. I had a recliner that I slept in right next to her. I think I was asleep for an hour when the inevitable happened. Kaia was having a full-blown night terror. She banged her head into the bars before I could get up to her. She was flailing about and had all her monitors and leads in a tangled mess. The nurse had to come in and help me untangle her. The night terrors persisted on and off throughout the night. The nurse tried giving her something for pain, but it didn't help. You could see her trying to get comfortable, but she was unsettled because she couldn't suck her thumb. From day one, she'd always sucked her right thumb to get to sleep. It's the only comfort item she always had, and now because of the arm restraints, she couldn't suck her thumb. It was a long stressful night that obviously brought back a lot of bad memories from surgery in China. It got me thinking, *Was there anyone to comfort and hold her after her surgery in China or was she left in her crib alone?* One thing I knew for sure—it was going to be a long six weeks.

The next morning Kaia looked better than I did. The attending pediatrician on call visited us; he clearly had a way with children and was able to get Kaia to smile. She was doing well from the surgical standpoint, and the only thing she was getting was oral pain medicine. She didn't even have an IV in anymore; it came out during one of the night terrors. She continued to drink from her cup without difficulties. Late morning, the surgeon came by to check on Kaia. He said everything looked good, and she'd be discharged tomorrow. The thought of another night in the hospital bed was dreadful, so I asked if there was a reason she couldn't be discharged that day. He looked at me, shrugged his shoulders, and said, "No, I guess not." We were on our way home two hours later!

The next few days were difficult. She was on a liquid diet for several days, then we were able to gradually advance to soft, mushy foods. She ate a lot of Jell-O and yogurt. I had worked so hard getting Kaia independent at feeding herself, now we had to feed her again for the next six weeks. We had to be careful feeding her. Basically we'd fill the spoon full of food and drop it into her mouth. It might have reminded you of feeding a baby bird.

Kaia was visibly irritated by the arm restraints. They wrapped around her arms from her wrists to shoulders. They were a soft material with a metal piece down the middle so they didn't bend. They were held together by Velcro and hooked together by a strap that went across her back. We were able to remove them for bath time, but we had to watch her like a hawk. As with any two-year-old, it takes less than a second for them to stick a toy or worse, her thumb, in her mouth. The poor thing looked like a penguin with her straight arms flapping about. Kids are resilient though, and she became quite adept at doing things with straight arms.

The nights were the worst. She wanted her thumb to suck, and with the arm restraints on, she couldn't sleep in her usual position, which made for a very unhappy Kaia. The first two weeks after surgery, she had night terrors every twenty to thirty minutes. I know it seems like I'm exaggerating, but I'm not. Kyle and I took turns getting up with her, but it didn't really matter as she never really woke up. I did eventually find that she did better if I woke her up during an especially long drawn-out episode. This is contrary to most recommendations, but you do what works best for your child. I knew if we could just take off her arm restraints, she'd sleep fine. After two weeks of little to no sleep, I took off her arm restraints to see if she'd sleep better. Sure enough, she curled up on her right side and slept like a baby. I didn't want to take the chance of her sucking her thumb, so I used medical tape and taped her thumb to her hand. I slept on her floor the rest of the night with no night terrors.

As the weeks wore on, Kaia became quite the escape artist when it came to getting out of her restraints. One morning I woke up in fear because we slept all night without a night terror. I was concerned something must be wrong with Kaia, and I ran into her room. She was lying in her bed sleeping with her restraints on the floor, Velcro still intact. It took a couple of days for us to figure out how she did it, but we think she wedged the top part of the restraint on the side of her bed and pulled her arm out. She must have nearly dislocated her shoulder doing it, but once one arm was out, she could easily pull the other side off. I have to give her credit for ingenuity. We made it through six weeks, and the doctor said the repair looked good. We still avoided any hard foods such as crackers and potato chips for a while, but her mouth was doing well. Probably the best Christmas present we gave her that year was taking off the restraints for good.

CHAPTER 8

The Next Two Years

Right before our eyes Kaia has blossomed into a beautiful little girl. However, just when Kaia seemed to finally trust us, and attachment and bonding were no longer an issue, we made a big parenting mistake. I've always said that finding good daycare for your children can be one of the most difficult tasks as a working parent. This point in our life proved no different. We made a change in our daycare situation that caused a major setback.

Because Kaia had to be driven to preschool and speech therapy sessions multiple times during the week, a traditional daycare setting was out of the question. We had a local woman who came to our home daily and provided in-home childcare for all three of our children. It worked out well, but when she had to quit for personal reasons, we were in a dilemma. When we couldn't find anyone right away, we opted to go with an au pair. For those of you not familiar with au pairs, they are usually young women in their twenties from foreign countries who want to live and study abroad. They provide childcare for your children, take a few college classes, and live in your home. It's similar to having a foreign exchange student except the au pair is considered an employee/childcare provider. We had two family members who had au pairs, and it worked well for them. From a financial standpoint, it wouldn't be any more expensive to have an au pair than to pay for daycare for three children, so we started the interviewing process.

Since Kaia was from China we decided to only interview young women from China. It seemed like the right thing to do. We could learn so much about Chinese culture and share our American customs with her. Kaia would have a native Chinese woman for a role model. She'd have someone to e-mail on Chinese holidays and ask questions about her culture when she got older. It seemed perfect. We were wrong. Our Chinese au pair, a twenty-four-year-old woman named Sabrina, arrived in our home ten months after bringing Kaia home. As soon as Sabrina arrived, Kaia went on the defensive. She wanted nothing to do with Sabrina. She'd refuse to let her do anything for her. If Kaia was thirsty, Sabrina would try to give her a glass of water, but Kaia wouldn't take it from her. When Kaia needed help getting dressed, she refused any assistance from Sabrina. Kaia started throwing more tantrums again and became very clingy to Kyle and me.

Obviously, Sabrina reminded her of her life in the orphanage and maybe Kaia feared that she would be taken away from us. We'll never know what was going through her little head, but we do know having a young Chinese woman in our home caused great stress and fear in our daughter. We all tried to make things work, but after about six months and for several different reasons, a mutual decision was made that Sabrina should be relocated with a new family in the area. It's unfortunate that we had to learn the hard way, but after the fact I've heard of other adoptive children that exhibited the same initial resentment to people of their same ethnicity. Since Sabrina left, we have been blessed with a new babysitter who has been invaluable to our family. She is a long-time family acquaintance and a grandmother herself. She lives nearby and comes to our house daily to transport Kaia to all of her appointments. Between the support of our babysitter, our parents, multiple family members, and friends, Kaia has become a very happy and well-adjusted child. The old saying, "It takes a village to raise a child" definitely rings true.

Following Kaia's original surgery, we started her in as much speech therapy as we could get. She went to speech therapy three to four times per week at first. It required a lot of driving on our part, but it was worth it to hear her start speaking. At first only Kyle and I could understand what few words Kaia spoke, but now complete strangers can understand her. She's starting to speak in short sentences, and her therapists are very happy with her progress. She's also getting a good grasp of the English language, but still not sure what certain things are called. Often she'll point at something and ask for it. When I ask her what it's called, she'll shrug her shoulders and say, "Umm, I dunno." At her most recent speech therapy evaluation, she continues to improve within the area of speech and language, but is still about twelve to twenty-four months behind her chronological age.

Since the original surgery, she's had two other surgeries; another set of tubes in the ears and a revision of a cleft palate repair, which also included an injection of fat into the soft palate to help with speech intelligibility. She still has a small fistula (hole) in the upper gum line that will require a much more extensive surgery including bone grafting to close the fistula. She will have this surgery at approximately age eight. After that surgery, then the oral surgeons and dentists will have their turn as her bite is off and her teeth are poorly aligned. Will it be difficult at times? Yes, but it could be much worse. Thankfully, Kaia's problems are all very correctable, and she is otherwise very healthy.

When she turned four, we enrolled her in a regular preschool program. I realize she was probably academically behind her peers, but she has been able to keep up. The most valuable aspect of preschool has been teaching Kaia social interaction. Growing up in an orphanage had resulted in very few manners and near complete lack of social skills. Originally, Kaia was very loud and often disruptive with constant interruptions, and she found it very difficult to share. It was also not uncommon to catch Kaia in a blatant lie. With the help of everyone involved, those behaviors are slowly disappearing. Kaia still has some troubles waiting her turn and is a bit on the hyperactive side, but she is acting more like a normal four-year-old every day. She will begin kindergarten in the fall. I'm well aware of the fact that she's still behind, but I'm optimistic that with one or maybe two years of kindergarten and extra work at home, she'll be back on track.

Motor development is no longer a worry. When she was still just three, I signed her up for a local dance class for three- and four-year-olds. Kyle thought I was crazy for starting her that year because he feared she wouldn't be able to keep up, but she proved him wrong. The first several weeks were difficult. She had troubles understanding the verbal instructions. Unless you spoke directly to Kaia, it went right over her head. Because of the speech and language delay, she learned much better by visual instruction.

She was so excited to go to dance class each week. She could hardly contain herself, which translated into a little girl that didn't stay in her spot very well. Kaia is quite the social butterfly, and you'd often see her leave her spot to go hug another one of the girls. I didn't expect her to master the steps, but she got much more out of the class than just tap and tumbling. When it came to the recital at the end of the year, I was skeptical as to how well she would do in front of so many people. Sitting there in the audience that night, I couldn't have been more proud that she is my daughter. She did the routine better than I'd ever seen her practice it, and she was a ball of excitement on that stage. She could see us in the audience and started jumping up and down yelling, "Hi, Mommy! Hi, Daddy!" When she did her tumbling routine, she was so excited, she reminded me of a racehorse at the starting gate. She had the crowd laughing. Her version of a cartwheel was a very fast somersault; you couldn't help but laugh. I had so many people tell me how much they enjoyed watching her. She's now in her second year of dance class and doing great. She is clearly functioning at the same skill level as the other girls in her group. I'm already looking forward to the next dance recital and the crazy antics I know to expect from Kaia.

Kaia may be smaller than her brothers, but she can hold her own. She's very muscular and loves to run and climb. This spring we were at a large playground and there was a rock-climbing wall for older kids to get to the slide. I looked over, and there was Kaia halfway up. She made it up without help. She's fearless most of the time. There was another little boy the same age as her, and he was too afraid to go on the bigger slides with Kaia. I swelled with pride as my little girl had not only caught up developmentally, but she was excelling. She loves to swim, and last summer went skiing behind our boat! Max did it, so she had to do it, too. She sat through her brothers' soccer games last season and each time begged to play. This year she is playing on her own soccer team. She is about a head shorter than the rest of the girls on the team but isn't intimidated in the least. At her first game, she managed to get her foot on the ball and kick it toward her goal. She got hit in the head but didn't start crying. She just rubbed her head and kept playing. With her only four-years-old, I couldn't ask for anything more.

Figure 10: Kaia water-skiing just after her fourth birthday!

Figure 11: Kaia on her first day of preschool.

Kaia's personality is the most striking of all. She's developed into a very loving child that is more than happy to give and receive affection. She's very compassionate. If I were to fall down and get hurt, she'd be first of my children to see if I were okay. She has fully attached and bonded to Kyle and me. It did take some time, but now nearly two and a half years later, I think that is no longer a concern. She is closest with Max. They play together well, and he has been an excellent role model for her. She has been very healthy and is finally over her eating issues. Just in the last month, she was able to leave the table with food still on her plate, and I've convinced her that she doesn't need to eat as soon as she wakes up in the morning. She no longer begs for food. She has realized she will not go hungry. She makes friends with everyone and has a zest for life. She has been described as defiant and by no means is she perfect, but what four-year-old is?

Thus far, being adopted hasn't been an issue for Kaia. She's almost five-years-old and has had very few questions about adoption. She knows that she was born in China but hasn't thought much beyond that point yet. In Kaia's mind, she's always been here in our family, and I'm her only mother. It hasn't occurred to her yet that she didn't grow in my tummy like her brothers did. As she grows older, we will surely be having some difficult conversations, and I can't help but feel unprepared. I wish I knew more. As I look at her brothers' baby books I can't help to feel saddened that Kaia will have more questions than answers about the first two years of her life. I've done everything I can to get her answers; we have photos of her finding spot thanks to our guide Frank, photos from the orphanage, and her finding ad—that's it. I have created a life book for her, which is basically a scrapbook including anything and everything about her adoption. This is as close to a baby book she will ever get. Kaia will want to know why her birthparents abandoned her. We can only speculate, but I truly believe that difficult decision was made in hopes that Kaia would receive the medical care she needed. I often think of her birthmother and hope that she somehow knows that Kaia is loved and doing well. More than anything, I hope Kaia knows that she is an integral part of our family, and we wouldn't be complete without her.

Finding Ads

When a child is found abandoned and taken to an orphanage, a finding ad is placed in the local newspaper. These ads usually include a picture of the child and location of the finding spot. It's a formal request for family to come forward and claim the child. The photographs in the finding ads are often taken at a younger age than the referral photos, thus may be the only chance of obtaining a baby photo of the adopted child. These finding ads are occasionally given to adoptive families at the time of adoption, but often they are not. There is an adoptive father here in the States who will find these ads for you at a cost of about $35. The Web site for this service is www.research-china.org.

We used the service, and he was able to find Kaia's finding ad, but the photo was the same as that in her referral photo; we estimate she was at least twelve-months-old in the photo. Nonetheless, it's still a valuable piece of her history.

Closing

When preparing to adopt internationally, I was amazed by the number of ignorant people who made the comment, "Oh, you're going to do it the easy way this time." Or comments like, "Gonna get a kid and a vacation out of it, too, huh?" It took every ounce of me not to blast them across the room. As a mom of children both biologically and through adoption, I'm here to tell you, it's anything but easy! I have to say it was much easier to have sex, incubate for nine months, and endure a few hours of physical pain. I realize that may seem cold, but when you have children biologically, no one inspects your home to make sure it's fit for children or requires all of your financial information to make sure you can afford a child. They don't fingerprint you and do background checks, or obtain letters of reference, or question you on your parenting skills. You don't have to deal with a child who has already gone through more losses and hardships than we will ever understand. If everyone had to go through this to have a child, Earth would be a much less populated planet. Is it just as rewarding? Yes.

It may seem like I have dwelled on the negative, but the fact of the matter is that it was very difficult the first two years. It took nearly two years before the orphanage behaviors disappeared. I felt like we had to "reprogram" her from the life that she knew. I believe she endured more hardship in her first two years of life than most of us will in a lifetime. Recovering from that takes time. Learning to trust and to love and be loved takes time. Our family is now at the point where we feel whole. It's hard to imagine our family without Kaia. All three of my kids have very different personalities, but each individual brings something unique to the group. I'm so glad that we persisted because I would have never forgiven myself if we didn't pursue our little girl. I would have lived with regret had we not adopted Kaia. The icing on the cake is that we were matched with such a wonderful child. I encourage families to pursue adoption both domestically and internationally because children deserve a home and a family to love them, but I caution you not to proceed with rose-colored glasses. It may not be easy at first, but the best things in life are worth fighting for!

Letter to My Daughter:

Dear Kaia,

If you are reading this, several years have passed since I wrote this book. I hope that you are not angry with me for sharing your story. I have shared some very intimate secrets and for that reason, I almost gave up on the idea more than once. However, the more I thought about it, it seemed like the right thing to do. You are such a happy child here in our family, and we feel so fortunate to have you. I'm sure you would hope that other children in orphanages would be offered that same blessing. This book was intended to help prepare those prospective adoptive families about to bring a precious child into their lives.

When you read through this story, please know that we never regretted our decision to adopt you. You and your brothers are the best things that have ever happened to your father and me. Life would not be complete without you. People often say that you are so lucky, but in reality, I am the lucky one. Thank you for all the joy that you already have and will continue to bring to our family. I love you to pieces!

Love,

Mom

Acknowledgments

I would like to thank several people for helping to make this book a reality. I want to thank not only those who helped me throughout the writing experience, but also those that helped during the adoption as the two go hand in hand.

First and foremost I need to thank my husband, Kyle. He is the love of my life, and without his support and encouragement, this adventure would not have been possible.

It was my father, Tom Miller, who taught me that if you want something badly enough, you'll find a way to make it happen. I thank you, Dad, for instilling those values in me. I think about you daily and miss you terribly.

My mother, Shirley Miller, has always been a constant support system for my family and me. I'd be lost without her. Kyle's parents, Chuck and Karen, have also been there anytime we needed them. All four of our parents have been excellent role models, and I can only hope that as parents ourselves, we will be equally great in the eyes of our children.

They say you can pick your friends but not your relatives. I'm happy to say that I have the cream of the crop with both. To my sibling and siblings-in-law: Mindy and Jeremy, Jason and April, Tim and Sara, and Kevin and Stacey, thank you for being so wonderful. I'm also blessed with my grandparents, Don and Rose, and Aunt Marilyn and Uncle Randy, who would do anything for my children. Special thanks to Cindy and Stacey for their editing skills, Jodi for her graphic design help, and to my friends for their encouragement with this project. I cherish my bond with each and every one of you. Every one of you has stepped up to the plate when we needed you to lean on, and I am honored to be a part of these wonderful families.

Many thanks to our adoption agency, Adoption Associates, Inc., which facilitated the entire process as seamlessly as possible.

Last but certainly not least, I thank my daughter, Kaia, because if it were not for her, this story would not exist. She is a fighter, strong and determined—an inspiration to anyone who knows her.

Made in the USA
San Bernardino, CA
22 December 2013